Jody Hilliard

HIGH-LIGHTS
OF THE
BIBLE

POETS and PROPHETS

A Bible Commentary for Laymen

Ray C. Stedman

Books

A Division of GL Publications
Ventura, California, U.S.A.

Other good reading:
Highlights of the Bible, Genesis-Nehemiah by Ray C. Stedman
Highlights of the Bible, New Testament by William L. Lane
What the Bible Is All About by Henrietta C. Mears

The foreign language publishing of all Regal books is under the direction of GLINT. GLINT provides financial and technical help for the adaptation, translation and publishing of books in more than 85 languages for millions of people worldwide.

For more information write: GLINT, P.O. Box 6688, Ventura, California 93006.

Published by Regal Books
A Division of GL Publications
Ventura, California 93006

Printed in U.S.A.
Library of Congress Card No. 81-50589
ISBN 0-8307-0774-3

Contents

A Teacher's Manual and Student Discovery Guide for
Bible study groups using this course are available from
your church supplier.

The Makeup of Man; The Character of God

The Bible is the most fascinating book in the world precisely because it answers the two most searching questions man can ask. The most profound question of all is: "Who is God?" What is He like—this strange invisible Being who created the world, governs the universe and holds in His hands the destiny of all creatures everywhere in all time. The second question is: "Who are we?" How did we get on this earth? Why are we put here? What is our relationship to the God who made us, and how can we find Him and know Him?

These are the questions which the Bible answers, but not by philosophical discourse, as the major books of other religions in the world attempt to do. Rather, the Bible reveals the self-disclosure of God through the events of history. It recounts the story of the creation of a physical earth on which is placed a human being whose reason for existence is to discover the marvels and majesty of the God who made him. Through disobedience a tragic separation occurs, and the rest of the book is the story of how God prepares man to recognize his helpless alienation and to understand how God Himself ultimately becomes flesh, the Eternal One becomes a temporal being like ourselves, that we may know the truth concerning ourselves.

We have already seen in volume one of *Highlights of*

the Bible, covering Genesis through Esther, that the Old Testament makes a special contribution to man's understanding of the redemptive plan of God. The divisions of the Old Testament reflect the several stages of this special contribution. The Pentateuch, the first five books of the Old Testament, develops the pattern of God's work with man, showing first, in Genesis, man's essential inadequacy without a close relationship with God. Exodus reveals God's grace in providing a redemptive act which will bring fallen man to Himself. Leviticus is the book of worship, teaching the means of access to God. Numbers describes the wandering of God's people through many up-and-down experiences, but always under the overarching, loving concern of the heavenly Father. Deuteronomy describes the faith which at last rests upon God's full ability to be all-in-all to His people.

The 12 historical books, from Joshua through Esther, depict the perils encountered along the spiritual journey of life. Though lived out in actual history, these stories are of great personal help to us for they picture the spiritual dangers we also face. There is the danger of premature contentment, reflected in the book of Joshua; the peril of dedicated blundering, found in the book of Judges; the peril of a forgotten calling, manifested in the stories of 1 and 2 Samuel; divided allegiance, described in the books of 1 and 2 Kings; the terrible peril of counterfeit faith, revealed in 1 and 2 Chronicles. Ezra, Nehemiah and Esther all describe the danger of the discouraged heart. Thus these books are given to us in order that we may see how to overcome such perils and recover from them.

This brings us then to the second half of the Old Testament which is also divided into two parts. There are the five poetical books—Job, Psalms, Proverbs, Ecclesiastes and Song of Solomon—which reflect both the rejoicings and the protests of man in response to life. There we find the sighs and the exaltations, the anger, contentment, tears and laughter of life. Though we call these books poetical this does not mean they are written in rhyme; rather it means they have a structure of repeated ideas expressed in magnificent language. This is the type of poetry the Hebrews employed.

Concluding this second division of the Old Testament are 17 books of the prophets: Five books of Major Prophets (designated so because of their size)—Isaiah, Jeremiah and his little volume of Lamentations, Ezekiel and Daniel; 12 books of Minor Prophets, so called because they are smaller in size. They record the prophetic messages of various men over the course of several centuries of time. Each of the prophetic books is built around a theme, revealing an attribute or character of God. For instance, Isaiah tells us how and why God redeems. Jeremiah speaks of how and why God chastens, while Ezekiel and Daniel describe how God rules. Thus in this second division of the Old Testament, as in the first, we find God and man together. Man discovers himself only when he begins to understand the self-disclosure of God.

Another fascinating feature of the Old Testament is that both of the divisions cover approximately the same span of time. The first division, beginning with Genesis, covers the early days of human history and the dawn of civilization. It ends with the books of Ezra, Nehemiah and Esther, which cover the return from captivity in Babylon during the fifth century B.C. The second division begins with the book of Job which takes us back again to the dawn of civilization. This division ends with the ministries of Haggai, Zechariah and Malachi, who were prophets of the post-exilic period following the return from Babylon, during which the Temple was being rebuilt and the city of Jerusalem reestablished. But the perspective of both divisions is quite different. The first division is much more external and deals with the facts recorded in history. The second division is more internal and deals with the changing, colorful passions of life. Here we touch on the feelings of the heart and the deep-seated, almost inexpressible yearnings and desires of the spirit. Though historical events are referred to in these books and form a framework for them, yet the central feature of the books is the deep probing of the inner recesses of human thought and the chronicle of the struggles and passions of man as he seeks to both resist and accept the will and purposes of God.

As already stated, the five poetical books reflect the passions and feelings of man, and since man is a three-fold being these five books fall into three divisions to correspond to the makeup of man: spirit, soul and body. The book of Job is perhaps the most profound and difficult book in the whole Bible. This is because it deals so penetratingly with the deepest part of our human makeup, the spirit within. As we shall soon see, no other book reveals so much of the nature of our humanity as the book of Job. It is the cry of the human spirit.

The three books of Psalms, Proverbs and Ecclesiastes together express the functioning of the human soul. Since the soul is the equivalent of our conscious life, it includes the faculties of mind, emotion and will, along with more minor distinctions such as conscience, memory, etc. The book of Psalms is essentially the book reflecting the emotions of God's people. It therefore voices our feelings. Proverbs details the continual choices which must be made throughout the journey of life, and the results that will accrue; it is therefore preeminently the expression of the will, while Ecclesiastes is the book given over to the logical searchings of the intelligence as to the meaning and purpose in life.

Finally, the book of the Song of Solomon has the distinction of being the only book in the Bible devoted to the praise and exaltation of the body. As Job is essentially the cry of faith, and Psalms, Proverbs and Ecclesiastes explore the hope of the human soul, the Song of Solomon deals with the glories of love, both from a physical and spiritual standpoint. Thus these poetical books probe the depths of the things which abide—faith, hope, and love. In doing so they remain forever a perennial source of fascinating exploration.

CHAPTER ONE

The Cry of the Spirit

JOB

The book of Job is perhaps the oldest book in the Bible. No one knows who wrote it. Some scholars think it may have been written by Moses while others date it as late as the time of Solomon. But one thing is certain: this book is given to us by the Holy Spirit. It is a beautiful and profound book, touching upon the themes of suffering more deeply than any other book in the Bible. It is also written in beautiful, majestic, even glorious language.

Job was a real man, not a mythological figure. He is mentioned by Ezekiel and is classified as one of the three great men of the Old Testament, along with Noah and Daniel. He is mentioned also in the New Testament by James, who refers to Job's patience and steadfast endurance. In the opening part of the book, Job is found living in the land of Uz, which is probably located in southeastern Edom. He is clearly one of the most prominent citizens of that land and may well have been a contemporary of Abraham. Thus the book takes us back to the very beginnings of biblical history.

Most of the book is poetry, but it begins and ends with prose sections which are like program notes given to an audience. Many scholars think this story was presented at times as a drama in which actors recited the parts of the different characters in the book.

Act I, God Meets with Angelic Creations

The book opens in heaven where God is meeting with the angelic creation. Among them is Satan who strides in sneering and swaggering, operating on the philosophy that self-interest is the only valid motive for all human behavior. In response God says: "Have you considered My servant Job? For there is no one like him on the earth, a blameless and upright man, fearing God and turning away from evil" (Job 1:8, *NASB*).

Some have felt that the book of Job is given us, for one reason, to help us understand the relationship between Satan and God. It is clear from this scene that Satan is not on an equal basis with God. Some scholars feel that the book of Job is the record of a great battleground between God and Satan, with Job caught in between. But what kind of battle is this in which one side must get permission from the other before it attacks? Can you imagine a German commander during World War II stepping up to General Patton, saluting him and saying, "Herr General, we would like permission to bomb your troops, destroy your tanks and wreck all your plans." Surely General Patton's reply would have been unprintable! Yet that is the situation we find in the book of Job. It is God who initiates a test of Job's character and proposes to Satan that Job be put to the test. Satan then responds with alacrity and asks permission from God to take away Job's prosperity so that he will curse God to His face.

The latter part of chapter 1 records the terrible results. One by one the props are pulled out from under Job's sense of well-being. In one tragic day Job learns that first all his oxen and donkeys were driven away by enemy raids and his servants slain. Next, word comes that his sheep have all been killed by a terrible electric storm, or perhaps a volcanic eruption. Crowding upon the heels of that comes the news that Job's great herd of camels, the true wealth of the oriental world, has been wiped out by a raid of Chaldeans. Finally comes the heart-rending news that his seven sons and three daughters were enjoying a birthday celebration together when a great tornado struck and the house was demolished and all his children killed. The malignancy of Satan is revealed in that he struck to the full extent of his permission. He went to the ultimate boundaries God had permitted and took away everything Job had.

Job's reaction to this is magnificent: "Then Job arose and tore his robe and shaved his head, and he fell to the ground and worshiped. And he said, 'Naked I came from my mother's womb, and naked I shall return there. The Lord gave and the Lord has taken away. Blessed be the name of the Lord' " (1:20,21, *NASB*).

It is clear that Job has won the first round of testing. Take away the possessions of a man like Job and he still will not curse God to His face. He still loves God and follows Him and recognizes God's right to do with him as He will.

But the test is not over. There is much worse yet to come. Before the book is finished we will see levels of pride in Job of which he is totally unaware, and we will begin to understand what God is after in Job's life (and in ours) by this kind of testing.

Again it is God that initiates further action against Job. Satan is rather taken aback by Job's steadfastness but responds to God's challenge by asking for a change in the rules. " 'Put forth Thy hand, now, and touch his bone and his flesh; he will curse Thee to Thy face.' So the Lord said to Satan, 'Behold, he is in your power, only spare his life' " (2:5,6, *NASB*).

So Satan is given renewed access to Job and without warning Job is suddenly stricken with a series of terrible boils or carbuncles. Some scholars think this was a form of leprosy. Others think it was a variety of elephantiasis which not only covers the body with running, putrifying sores, but also causes swelling and distortion. Whatever it was it rendered Job a pitiful spectacle; a repulsive hulk of a man, swollen, disfigured and hurting.

As the malady continues, Job's wife is the first whose faith succumbs. She turns on him and says, "Do you still hold fast your integrity? Curse God and die" (2:9, *NASB*).

Just as Satan used Eve as his instrument to get at Adam in the Garden of Eden, so the assault upon Job's emotional life comes through his wife's failure of faith. She advises him to do two things: apostatize and then commit suicide.

But once again Job's faith proves triumphant. He gently rebukes his wife and reasserts the right of God to be sovereign in human affairs. Job's wife had the philosophy that life ought to be pleasant, and if it was not there was no use living. Job at least understands that the reason we are on earth is not necessarily to have a good time. When the pressure comes, life is still worth living. Job argues that we take God's joy and pleasure with gladness and gratitude. If He then chooses to send something difficult, shall we abandon the gratitude and begin to curse Him in protest? To do so is to allow Satan the victory.

Clearly Job has won again. The score is now 2-0 in favor of Job. But Satan is not through. He had obtained permission from God to assault this man in every area of his being. He has taken away Job's possessions and all his children, and now he has taken away also his health and the pleasure of living, even to the degree of making Job feel abandoned by his wife.

Satan now proceeds to attack the final stronghold of Job's spirit. In the closing verses of chapter 2 he moves up his heavy artillery, and the big guns he seeks to employ are, to say the least, most unexpected and unusual. "Now when Job's three friends heard of all this adversity that had come upon him, they came each one from his own place, Eliphaz the Temanite, Bildad the Shuhite, and Zophar the Naamathite; and they made an appointment together to come to sympathize with him and comfort him" (v. 11, *NASB*).

At this point the whole book slightly shifts its focus. We no longer are looking only at Job but now at his controversy with these three friends, and their discourses occupy the major part of the book. The primary attack on Job's faith now comes not alone through his physical trials but through an attack on his spiritual relationship with God by means of these three well-meaning friends.

When the friends arrive they are shocked at what they see. They can hardly believe their eyes. This monstrous, repulsive hulk of a man—could he really be their dear old friend Job? Could this obnoxious creature sitting on a heap of ashes, scraping himself with a broken piece of pottery, be the man they had known and loved? They tear their coats, sprinkle dust on their heads in oriental mourning, and finally end up sitting on the ground around Job observing him in silence for seven days.

While they were sitting there they were thinking, and what they thought will come out in the arguments they present in the next section of the book. It is enough for us to see at this point that while they were waiting in silence around Job they came to the conclusion that he was suffering under the hand of God for some terrible sin he must have committed and that it was therefore right for God to make him suffer this way. Their hearts were hardening against Job. They had come to comfort him, but in their heart of hearts they believed that Job deserved what he was getting.

Act II, Dialogue with Three Friends

There are three cycles of dialogue with Job and his

friends. They try various approaches with Job: first, sarcasm and irony; then they appeal to Job's honesty; finally they accuse him of specific crimes and misdeeds, and in the end fall silent and sit miffed and sulking because they feel Job has insulted them. In all their speeches they attack Job's integrity with the argument that if God is indeed just, the righteous are always blessed and the wicked suffer. If an individual is suffering, it must therefore be because something is wrong in his life. Their explanation of suffering is a simple matter of cause and effect. It is neat and tidy and explains everything—that is, unless you happen to be the sufferer!

Before the dialogue begins, Job raises three questions. It is evident that after months of suffering a change has taken place in him. He no longer submits without question to the will of God, but begins to ask why. First, "Why was I ever born?" His misery is so intense that he would like to have his birth day blotted out of existence and left unrecorded on the calendar. His second question is, "Why didn't I die at birth?" Life has been totally meaningless, Job infers, and it would have been better to have died at birth. Then he gives his view of death as a time of rest and quiet after the tumult and trouble of life. His third question is: "Why can't I die now?" He is not thinking of suicide, but only desires that God would take his life.

After Job asks these questions the first cycle of the replies of the friends is introduced. Though these friends propose the same solution to the problem of suffering they approach it in three distinct ways, according to their personalities. They might be nicknamed Eliphaz the Eloquent, Bildad the Brutal, and Zophar the Zealous.

Eliphaz, the first speaker, is evidently the oldest, for there is a smoothness about him and a courtesy (at least at the beginning) that indicates he has learned to say unpleasant things in gracious ways. His first argument breaks down into six main points. He begins in chapter 4 by saying, in effect, "Follow your own advice, Job. You have been a counselor to many and you have been able to put your finger on their problem and help them deal with it. You delivered them and found the key to what was troubling them, and now your turn has come. Follow your own advice and you will be relieved." His second point is that the basic principle of life is that the righteous are never punished; only the unrighteous suffer. Eliphaz goes on to tell Job that if he will fear God and admit his sin, things will be all right. He claims to have learned this truth from a vision in which he saw that God is of such holiness and purity that even the angels stand defiled before Him. What chance can a man have, then, to claim sinlessness? Though this is accurate theology it is unbalanced, for it sees God only as a God of justice and knows nothing of His love, compassion and forgiveness nor of the discipline and training of the Father's heart.

In chapter 5 Eliphaz argues that trouble comes only from sin, and he slyly suggests that the loss of Job's children was the result of Job's personal evil. He then warns Job not to play games with God because God knows too much. Finally he closes with a section which says, in effect, "Just give up and God will bless you."

Job's reply to this is found in chapters 6 and 7. In chapter 6 Job rebukes his friends, stating that he has a right to complain because of his terrible suffering. "For the arrows of the Almighty are in me; my spirit drinks their poison; the terrors of God are arrayed against me" (6:4).

Then he speaks of his inability to bear more pain. "What does God think I am made of, stone or bronze that He subjects me to all this?" (see 6:12).

Then Job expresses his irritation at the misunderstanding of his friends. He says in effect, "You friends are like the mountain brook that is full of water in the wintertime when no one needs it, but when the hot summer sun comes out and we long for the refreshing of the water, it is nothing but a dry, gravel-filled streambed. You said you came to comfort me and all you have given me is trouble."

Job then turns to God and complains to Him about the hardness of his present experience. He views the future as absolutely hopeless, and in the honesty of his despair, in baffled bewilderment, he cries, "Have I sinned? What have I done to Thee, O watcher of men? Why hast Thou set me as Thy target, so that I am a burden to myself?" (7:20, *NASB*).

In chapter 8 the second friend takes up the attack. His name is Bildad the Shuhite, but we have called him Bildad the Brutal. His style is to ask questions in an effort to focus everything into logical framework. He is a cold intellectual thinker who debates the issue at the level of the mind.

His first question is, "Can God do wrong?" He feels that Job has slandered God and he moves on from his basic premise to draw the logical conclusion, "If your children have sinned against God He has delivered them into the power of their transgression. When they died on that tragic day you can only conclude it was because they did something terribly wrong." He supports his argument further by various platitudes of the day, pointing out how God always cuts off those who seem to prosper because of evil in their midst, and he closes with an exhortation to Job to repent.

Job replies to Bildad in chapters 9 and 10. He explains the difficulty he has with God, for he accepts the principle that trouble comes only because of sin. He would have analyzed another's problems along the same line before his own trials began, but in the long dark hours of searching his own heart he has not been able to put his finger upon any sin he has not already dealt with. His dilemma is, "I am not aware of sin in myself, yet I am in deep trouble; therefore, the problem must lie in God." But he has no way of examining God, and he states this in very eloquent terms. God's wisdom is far beyond man's and He exercises power which can only make man tremble in awe. His invisibility makes it difficult to deal with Him and His sovereignty is overwhelming. "If I called and He answered me, I could not believe that He was listening to my voice. For He bruises me with a tempest, and multiplies my wounds without cause" (9:16,17, *NASB*).

He goes on to describe how life becomes incomprehensible when there is no understanding of God. The reference point is then gone and one cannot make any sense of life. But in verses 33 through 35, out of the deep darkness that surrounds this suffering saint, a ray of light breaks through. It represents the first awareness of what is missing. "There is no umpire between us, who may lay his hand upon us both. Let Him remove His rod from me, and let not dread of Him terrify me. Then I would speak and not fear Him; but I am not like that in myself" (*NASB*).

Job at last begins to feel, deep in his bones, the terrible gulf between man and God that must be bridged by another. God is laying the foundation in Job's understanding for the tremendous revelation which comes in the New Testament: God at last becomes Man.

But in chapter 10 the darkness closes in again around Job. He pleads with God to let him know what is wrong, or at least to leave him alone, for anything is better than his present misery.

Every argument which has ever occurred to a suffering saint is brought out here in the book of Job. Every nuance of suffering, whether mental or physical, is explored to its utmost throughout the book. All the tormenting questions are asked. All the haunting dilemmas are faced, so that anyone who is suffering will find that Job has felt whatever he has felt and has articulated it eloquently. The questions are not answered at this point, but they will be answered before we are through, yet in a way we could never anticipate.

In chapter 11 Zophar the Naamathite (we can call him Zophar the Zealous) moves up to bat and opens with a scorching rebuke to what he sees as Job's sinful folly. He accuses Job of wordiness, foolishness, mockery and of self-righteous smugness. He says Job is only getting what is coming to him and not even all of that. He describes Job's stupid ignorance in contrast with God's deep wisdom and inscrutable ways. He closes with the shining possibilities that are ahead if Job will only repent.

The problem with these friends is that though much of their theology is correct, yet they answer Job's words without trying to find out what lies behind them. They comment on what he says without understanding his agony. Further, though their theology is correct as far as it goes, it is very incomplete. They speak with the utmost confidence that what they are saying is the final word on the subject. There is apparently no understanding that perhaps there are aspects of God and dimensions to His wisdom that they have not yet seen. The third thing wrong is that they never pray with Job. They never ask God for help to open their minds and illuminate their understanding so they can help their friend. The book is filled with prayers, but they are all prayers of Job crying out to God in the midst of his sufferings.

This is the difference between mere theology and the experience of a man taught by the Spirit. Theology can be very clear and right, but when one is dealing with the hurting problems of life a deeper dimension must be added—that compassion Jesus manifested, that sympathy that identifies with hurt and opens the door of the spirit to receive more light.

The first round ends with Job's sarcastic defense, found in chapters 12 through 14. Job sees his friends as know-it-alls who deal with elementary truths which everyone knows. Consequently they have not helped him but are really in the same boat with him, being subject to the same judgments from God that they warn him about. He therefore requests they leave him alone with God, and only asks they will do him the courtesy of listening carefully to the case he seeks to present before Jehovah.

In chapter 13 Job is like a man in prison, planning his case for his appearance before God. He divides his case into four major points. The first is a plea for certain conditions he feels must be granted before he can talk with God. One is that God will lift the pain and anguish he is now going through so he does not have to speak out of torment. Second, that God would so veil His presence that Job will not be terrified by His awesomeness.

He next pleads for the knowledge of the charges which are against him, and protests the silence of God in His apparent anger with him. In chapter 14 in two marvelously moving passages, Job brings out the helplessness and hopelessness of man before God. Job feels that man is helpless to control his affairs but God judges this limited helpless man for things he cannot help. Because of his sense of hopelessness, he cries out for a kind of purgatory after life is finished. He sees life only as a natural man, with the present existence as the only truly important thing, and if one does not make something out of the present experience he will never have another chance. So the first cycle of dialogue ends with Job's stout insistence that he has done no wrong, so he cannot understand what is behind his torment.

Act III, Second Round of Speeches

In chapters 15-21, the second round of speeches is recorded. For this the friends gird up their loins, sharpen their spears and come at Job again. Once again Eliphaz the Eloquent is the first speaker. He charges Job with presumptuous words and with pretentious claims, and then supports it with his narrow and worn out theology. He points out the general nature of the depravity of man and the effects of the Fall upon human life. He rightly says that there is no one who is clean and righteous before God, but he fails to point out specifically what it is that Job has done. As a matter of fact he himself is guilty of the very thing he sets before Job because he too is part of the human race, yet there is never a word of self-examination from him.

In a long passage Eliphaz argues again from experience, pointing out that God will never let a man get by with wickedness, and therefore if one is being punished he must be wicked. It is the same old tired thrust at Job: he must be guilty of some terrible sin.

In chapters 16 and 17 Job answers Eliphaz. He does not really know what to say, but he is trying to be honest. The great thing about Job is that he is no hypocrite. He never tries to cover over or set his case in a better light than it truly is. He simply blurts out all the hurt and anguish of his heart as best he can.

Again he rebukes his friends for their misunderstanding and windy words. Though Job cannot see it, it is clear to us that Satan is there in the background using these friends as channels for what the apostle Paul calls "the fiery darts of the wicked one" (see Eph. 6:16). It is a good reminder to beware lest we become a channel for Satan's accusations against someone who is suffering as Job is suffering here.

Job goes on to state the facts as he now sees them. He can only conclude that God must hate him, though he does not know why, for He lets men insult him and seems to totally disregard Job's innocence. Despite these strong feelings a gleam of faith emerges at this point in that Job still sees that God must supply the answers to these questions, for man is totally helpless to solve them in his ignorance. Job concludes this reply by praying for relief, largely from his friends. He has heard all their arguments and knows they do not help, and in the final part of chapter 17 he sinks back again into the darkness of despair.

Bildad the Brutal then takes up the cudgels with the same tired line of argument as before. He is a good example of what has been described as "an evangelical crab." To this attack Job replies with a piteous plea. He beseeches mercy from his friends and describes his own bafflement at what is happening to him. His feelings of isolation from all are very vivid. "My breath is offensive to my wife, and I am loathsome to my own brothers. Even young children despise me; I rise up and they speak against me. All my associates abhor me, and those I love have turned against me" (19:17-19, *NASB*).

But once again faith responds and he utters the great anticipation of bodily resurrection for which he is famous: "I know that my Redeemer [Vindicator] lives, and at the last He will take His stand on the earth. Even after my skin is flayed, yet without my flesh I shall see God; whom I myself shall behold, and whom my eyes shall see and not another" (19:25-27, *NASB*).

Slowly, through the anguish and gloom of this man's heart born out of passion and pathos, comes the dawning realization that God is working out a great and mighty purpose, and that one of these days God Himself (whom Job has never failed to see as the God of great majesty and power) will be visibly present before men. Thus with a slow but certain light, Job is gradually learning that though life is essentially a mystery, God is working out His own purposes.

Job ends the discourse by warning his friends to be careful about judging him. "If you say, 'How shall we persecute him?' and 'What pretext for a case against him can we find?' then be afraid of the sword for yourselves, for wrath brings the punishment of the sword, so that you may know there is judgment" (19:28,29, *NASB*).

Despite Job's tremendous flash of hope, Zophar the Zealous looses a blast of impassioned words in a strong outburst of emotions against Job. These three men represent what the New Testament would call *pharasaism*—an appearance of being orthodox, yet without true godliness. Pharasaism is one of the most deadly enemies of truth, for it is so easily self-deceptive. Chapter 20 represents Zophar's last appearance in the book. His argument is that the prosperity of the wicked is always short and his joy is but for a moment. He goes on to describe the punishment of the wicked as being terrible and always certain.

Job's response this time is very reasoned and calm. Though sometimes he speaks rather sharply to his friends, at other times, perhaps when the pain is not as intense, he is able to speak more dispassionately. After a reasoned appeal for a careful hearing, Job sets forth the facts about the wicked. They often live lives that are for the most part untroubled. They openly defy God and yet prosper. God's judgments upon them are infrequent and long delayed, and even when they come they seem to be uneven. He concludes the second cycle of dialogue by chiding his friends for their hidden surmises and their unsupported convictions. His closing words are: "How then will you vainly comfort me, for your answers remain full of falsehood?" (21:34, *NASB*).

Act IV, Final Round of Speeches

The third and final round of speeches is found in chapters 22 through 31. Eliphaz begins the round again, but whereas once he had been calm and courteous he now is clearly upset and angry, and begins to pour out invective and accusation upon poor Job. He accuses Job of imaginary motives and even stoops to inventing totally false charges against Job. In a rather patronizing way, he assumes insulting concepts which he feels Job holds and ends with inappropriate exhortations (though phrased in beautifully expressive language) to Job to confess his sin and return to God, with the hope that God will again pour out blessings upon him.

In a most moving reply Job does not attempt to answer the arguments of his friends any further. He simply cries out of a troubled heart, expressing before them but addressed to God, the deepest problem he now feels. He has two basic questions: Why is God absent and Why is God silent? As Job's pain increases and his frustration grows, his basic longing for God remains, and though he searches everywhere to find God nothing seems to work. Yet despite this, a slowly growing faith in God's justice sustains him and confidence in God's ultimate purpose encourages him. Nevertheless, he is terribly afraid of God and dreads a confrontation with Him. It is in this section that his progressing faith produces the highest expression of trust found in the book. "But He knows the way I take. When He has tried me, I shall come forth as gold" (23:10, *NASB*).

In chapter 24 Job faces his second question: Why is God silent? He raises the complaint many have raised about God, Why doesn't He judge evil? Job points out that thieves and scoundrels flourish, poor people suffer terribly, having to scratch for a living, being exposed to the elements and exploited by the rich and yet seem neglected by God. Criminals strike in the darkness and yet God delays His justice. Thus, though the three friends assert that evil finds invariable retribution, Job points out that the facts of life are quite different.

In a final blunt address, Bildad the Brutal restates his argument that God is all-powerful and man is inherently sinful. Then he concludes: "How then can a man be just with God? Or how can he be clean who is born of woman? If even the moon has no brightness and the stars are not pure in His sight, how much less man, that maggot, and the son of man, that worm!" (25:4-6, *NASB*).

In chapter 26, Job concludes the dialogue with the friends. His answer to Bildad is one rich in irony. He sarcastically declares that the friends have been of no help at all to him, for he quite agrees that there is a mystery in God that no man can plumb. Even when man recognizes God's omnipresence, omnipotence and omniscience, still he cannot explain all of God's ways.

In a closing soliloquy, covering chapters 27 through 31, Job reviews the situation. He states again his sense of unshakeable integrity, for there are facts he cannot deny and yet he must agree with much his friends have stated. In a passage of moving beauty he traces man's search for wisdom, comparing it with the hardships men endure in mining the mountains for treasures of gold and silver. He concludes that wisdom is illusive for it cannot be found by searching, cannot be purchased with gold and cannot be known in nature. The only way to obtain it, he asserts, is from God, for God knows what it is, where it is and how to find it.

In painful reminiscence, Job looks back on the good old days of his prosperity and blessing, recounting in detail the honor that was shown him and the power of his influence over others. He contrasts that with the painful present where he faces the mockery of men, the anguish of pain and—the ultimate torment—the silence of God. But once again he searches his life for a clue as to why he is being so tormented. There have been, he says, no sexual misdeeds, no injustice toward his servants or the poor, no trust in wealth, no secret idolatry, no gloating over other's misfortunes, no stinginess or hypocrisy and no polluting or misuse of his land. He can find no reason in himself why God continues to allow this pain to go on.

With this, the words of Job are ended. He has nothing further to say. Baffled, questioning, tormented, yet unwilling to forsake God, he falls silent.

Act V, The Man from Buz

At this point a noteworthy break in the book occurs. Another voice is heard, that of a young man named Elihu. He is identified as the son of Barachel (which means "God blesses") the Buzite.

In the opening of the book we learn that Job lived in the land of Uz, but there was a nearby land called Buz. These two lands were named for two brothers who lived in the days of Noah following the flood. Elihu came from the land of Buz.

Commentators seem to differ widely in their view of Elihu. Some regard him as a brash young man, speaking out of the cocksure arrogance of youth, who tells the older men how they are wrong. Others see him as merely repeating the arguments of the three friends without adding much to them. Still other commentators view Elihu's discourse as a kind of meaningless interruption, of which God takes no notice at all. But still others (with whom I agree) see Elihu as playing a very important part in this book.

It is noteworthy that at the end of the book when God rebukes the friends of Job, Elihu is not included. Also he is given a very prominent part in the drama. His message occupies the next five chapters and constitutes one of the major discourses of the book. And he always speaks with courtesy and sensitivity to Job, despite his strong feelings. He seems to recognize the depth of Job's suffering and always speaks with understanding. Probably the most important thing about Elihu is that he claims to speak not out of experience as the other men did, but from revelation. He claims that "the Almighty gives [man] understanding" (32:8, *NASB*).

Elihu, therefore, comes into the book as the answer to Job's cry for an explanation. God replies to Job in a way he did not expect, for suddenly a young man who has been listening all along speaks up and appears as witness to the

Mediator for whom Job has been asking throughout the book. Elihu thus appears as a kind of John the Baptist of the Old Testament. He begins where the friends began, but ends with words very similar to the voice of God when God ultimately appears on the scene.

In chapter 32, with a courteous word of explanation, Elihu states that he has not entered the discussion before because he felt his youth might make his judgments seem immature, but now since old age has not solved the problem of Job's suffering he feels pressured to speak. He opens with an invitation to Job to dialogue with him, promising that he will give only honest words and speak without partiality.

Then in 33:8 Elihu begins to analyze Job's view of God. He says Job sees God as capricious, acting as men do out of His feelings and moods; and his answer is that in this Job is not right, for God is much greater than man. Further, Elihu says, Job claims that God is silent, but actually God speaks in two ways: (1) in dreams and (2) in pain, even repeating Himself patiently so that man may get the message. The essence of Elihu's argument is that affliction is sent by a God of love in order to discipline and purify. To this Job is invited to reply, but he remains silent.

In chapter 34 Elihu goes on to take up Job's view of God in further detail, opening with an invitation to all who listen to join in the judgment. Elihu claims that though Job is patient with his attackers, nevertheless his view of God makes him echo the arguments of the ungodly: "What man is like Job, who drinks up scoffing like water, who goes in company with evildoers and walks with wicked men? For he has said, 'It profits a man nothing that he should take delight in God' " (34:7-9).

In effect, Elihu says Job is saying, "What advantage is it to me to behave myself? I might as well have sinned." But in a powerful passage Elihu reveals the truth about the character of God. He cannot be unjust because He cannot deny Himself, and since He judges men He Himself must be just. Further, He is beyond accountability to man, for no man authorized Him to act and nothing functions without Him. Actually it is He who teaches man what justice is, for man cannot govern without the concept of justice and he learns impartial justice from observing God. Yet God does not need to investigate when He judges and will not accept outward reformation, but requires inward repentance. Therefore, the consensus of the wise is that Job speaks from some degree of ignorance of God and needs further enlightenment.

Chapters 36 and 37 conclude Elihu's argument by presenting a magnificent description of the glory of God. He begins with a claim to speak from divine authority, saying: "For truly my words are not false; One who is perfect in knowledge is with you" (36:4, *NASB*). Some commentators have thought that he is referring to himself as "perfect in knowledge" and is therefore a brash and arrogant young man.

But in chapter 37, verse 16, he asks Job: "Do you know about the layers of the thick clouds, the wonders of one perfect in knowledge . . . ?" (*NASB*). Obviously he here refers to God and his claim, therefore, in chapter 36 is that he is speaking with the wisdom and authority of God, who is perfect in knowledge.

He points out that Job is in a rather perilous position because he is so preoccupied with justice that he comes close to blasphemy and judgment in his view of God. If he goes on in this vein his case will be hopeless, for God's wisdom is inscrutable and He is varied in His purposes, being great in power and justice, and unimpressed by man's conceit.

Act VI, God's Message to Job

This brings us to the climax of the book of Job, where

the voice of Jehovah Himself is heard, speaking out of the whirlwind. In the first of God's two speeches to Job He sets forth a series of questions designed to test Job's competence to argue with the Almighty. The language and poetic style of this passage is magnificent, unequalled in all of literature.

Jehovah first asks concerning the earth, as to where Job was when its foundations were laid. And then selecting its most prominent feature, the sea, God proceeds to question Job as to how the sea was born and how it is kept within limits. He probes Job's understanding on the processes of day and night and what lies beneath the sea and beyond the boundaries of life and behind the horizons of history. He continues to ask about common mysteries, such as the source of light, the uses of snow and hail and the processes of the storm and ice and frost.

Then He explores the heavens, questioning Job as to his power to bring forth the spring, symbolized by the Pleiades; or the winter season, represented by Orion; or to control the Zodiac or the influence of the Great Bear in the north. Finally He examines Job's ability to handle God's daily chores of feeding the animals, watching over their birth processes, giving them varied instinctive controls— the wide-ranging freedom of the wild ass, the independence of the wild ox, the stupidity of the ostrich, the courage of the horse and the vision of the hawk and the eagle.

In reply to all this, Job admits his total incompetence to contend with the Almighty and declares himself unwilling to speak further. But though he is silenced, he is not yet convinced. He has not discovered yet the basic problem of his life or learned what God had in mind when He invited Satan to try him in the first place. So, in Jehovah's second speech out of the whirlwind He uses two symbolic beasts to teach Job the final truth he needs to learn. Once again he subjects Job to a series of questions, but this time as to his ability to morally govern the world and mankind. "Look on everyone who is proud, and humble him; and tread down the wicked where they stand. Hide them in the dust together; bind them in the hidden place. Then I will also confess to you, that your own right hand can save you" (40:12-14, *NASB*).

In the next sections God brings before Job two amazing animals, one called Behemoth, a land animal; and one called Leviathan, a sea creature. Commentators have had difficulty identifying these in the natural world. Some think Behemoth is either the hippopotamus or the elephant, perhaps even the rhinoceros. They feel that Leviathan is the crocodile, though some think it could be a whale. But the language employed here clearly goes beyond the natural realm. These beasts seem to be symbolic of that which is invisible and supernatural. Behemoth, the land animal, means in Hebrew "beasts," and Leviathan means "the folded one." Isaiah in chapter 27 refers to Leviathan thus: "In that day the Lord will punish Leviathan the fleeing serpent, with His fierce and great and mighty sword, even Leviathan the twisted serpent; and He will kill the dragon who lives in the sea" (v. 1, *NASB*).

This brings to mind the two beasts found in Revelation 13, one which comes from the sea and reigns over the waters, representing the multitudes of the people of the earth. The other beast comes out of the land; but behind both is still a third creature called the Great Dragon, and we are told plainly that he is Satan who gives his power and authority to the Beast. Thus, here in Job, we have a tie to the opening scene of the book where Satan appears before God and is given authority over the life of Job. Behemoth represents the Satanic twist in man's fallen nature against which we all struggle and which the Bible calls "the flesh," with its continual desire to assert itself and live for itself. The second beast represents the world with its vast influence upon each of us, pressuring us to conform to its philosophies and reflecting the values and attitudes of a satanic view of life.

One Bible commentator has put it this way: "It seems probable that Behemoth represents the evil one acting in the animal and carnal elements of man's own constitution, and that Leviathan symbolizes the evil one energizing as man's external enemy. Behemoth is the enemy within us. Leviathan is the enemy without us."

In magnificent poetry, these two supernatural animals are described. Behemoth is viewed as self-sufficient, self-centered and totally self-confident; while Leviathan appears as untameable, unconquerable in his fierceness, fearful and awe-inspiring, irresistible in strength, and yet characterized totally by pride. The secret of his life is revealed in Job 41:33,34: "Nothing on earth is like him, one made without fear. He looks on everything that is high, he is king over all the sons of pride" (*NASB*).

These are the beasts that Job is up against. God's question is: "Job, are you able to handle these?" Job is here given a clear revelation of the reason behind his illness. Not his own failure or willful misdeeds, but a serious problem so imbedded in his nature that he is not even aware that it exists, yet it is destroying him. It is with this God must deal.

Chapter 42 sets forth Job's repentance, consisting of a new view of God Himself and a totally new view of his own life. He says in response to God's charges, "You're right, Lord. I have been ignorant" (see v. 3), and again, "You're right, Lord. I have been arrogant" (see vv. 4,5). He concludes: "I have heard of Thee by the hearing of the ear; but now my eye sees Thee; therefore I retract, and I repent in dust and ashes" (42:5,6, *NASB*).

Thus Job learns that the ultimate problem of life is within us, but it is a problem that only God can handle. We are unable, totally unequipped to handle it by ourselves. All we can do is put ourselves in His gracious hands and allow Him to work out the circumstances of our lives, to teach us what He desires us to learn. This is surely what Jesus has in mind in the Sermon on the Mount: "Blessed are the poor in spirit, for theirs is the kingdom of heaven" (Matt. 5:3).

The closing scenes of the book record Jehovah's rebuke of the friends and His vindication of Job before them. They are required to bring an offering of sacrifice and to request Job to make intercession for them before their sin is forgiven and set aside.

The book closes with Jehovah's complete restoration of Job, granting him double blessing in all that he once possessed, including even seven more sons and three more daughters. Job's closing days are recorded: "And after this Job lived 140 years, and saw his sons, and his sons' sons, four generations. And Job died, an old man, full of days."

CHAPTER TWO

The Voicing of Feelings

PSALMS

The book of Psalms joins with Proverbs and Ecclesiastes in expressing the cry of man's soul. Just as the soul has three major divisions—the emotions, mind and will—so these books express these divisions. The primal need of the human spirit is faith, because man was made to believe in God, but the cry of the human soul is for hope.

The book of Psalms particularly reflects the variety of human hopes. Every experience of man's heart is reflected here. No matter what mood you find yourself in, some psalm will reflect that mood, for this amazing book records every one of man's emotions and reactions. Some people seem to have discovered the secret of perpetual emotion; these people certainly ought to get well acquainted with the book of Psalms! For instance, if you are fearful read Psalm 56 or Psalm 91, or certainly Psalm 23, the famous Shepherd Psalm which everyone knows. If you are discouraged read Psalm 42 which is only one among many for the discouraged. If you happen to be feeling lonely, then turn to Psalm 71 or Psalm 62.

If you are oppressed by sinfulness there are two marvelous psalms for this: Psalm 51 written after David's double sin of adultery and murder, and Psalm 32, also

David's great expression of confession and forgiveness.

If you find yourself worried or anxious I would recommend Psalm 37 and Psalm 73. If you are angry, try Psalm 13 or Psalm 58. If you are resentful, Psalm 94 or Psalm 77. If you find yourself feeling happy and wanting words to express your happiness, read Psalm 92 or Psalm 66. If you feel forsaken, try Psalm 88. If you are grateful and would like to say so, read Psalm 40. If you are doubtful and you find faith is beginning to fail, read Psalm 119.

A few years ago I entered a house and stumbled upon the body of a man who had committed suicide. I found the body lying in a pool of blood. What a shock it was! I had known him fairly well for he had been coming to me for counseling help. That night I found it impossible to sleep because I was so disturbed and troubled. In that hour of desolation my wife and I turned to Psalms and read some of them together. It was the only book that could quiet our hearts in an hour of trouble and anguish. Psalms has always been the book where men and women of God have pillowed their heads in times of distress or heartache and sorrow. Whatever your feeling, turn to Psalms.

Many people think of Psalms as being entirely the work of King David, but in fact, though more than half of them were written by David, the sweet singer of Israel, there are several authors besides him and many of the psalms are anonymous. Most of them were written to be sung in public, which is why you will often find at the beginning of the psalm "to the chief choirmaster." In some Bibles the Hebrew titles are given which are normally translated either as psalms, prayers or praises. One psalm (90) was written by Moses and one by King Solomon (127). There are also psalms by Asaph who was the chief choirmaster under King David, and a group of psalms is attributed to the Sons of Korah, who were a band of musicians charged with leading the singing of Israel. Thus the psalms were written over a long period of time, beginning with the days of Moses and including the return of Israel from exile in Babylon.

No one knows who collected the psalms, but the final collection of 150 psalms constitutes the longest book in the Bible and was divided from antiquity into five books, each ending with a doxology (praise to God). You will find the first one at the end of Psalm 41 which closes the first book and reads: "Blessed be the Lord, the God of Israel, from everlasting to everlasting! Amen and Amen."

Similar doxologies are found at the end of the other books: Book II from Psalm 42 to 72; Book III Psalm 73 to 89; Book IV Psalm 90 to 106; and Book V Psalm 107 to 150. Among the Jews the book of Psalms was closely associated with the Pentateuch, the five books of Moses, and this may well represent a key to the structure of the book of Psalms.

As we have seen repeatedly, the five books of Moses were designed deliberately to give us a pattern of God's working in human history in the world of nations and with individuals. The five books of Psalms follow the same pattern, but reflect the emotional reactions of the heart to God's divine program. This explains the fact that has troubled many about Psalms. Certain psalms (called impreeatory psalms) speak with bitter, scorching words against enemies, calling down God's wrath upon them and wishing the enemies to be torn limb from limb and hung from the nearest tree. This disturbs many who feel the message of Psalms is much different from the New Testament with regard to loving our enemies and our treatment of them.

Other psalms give the impression that human existence ends with death and there is no afterlife, but we must remember that the psalms reflect the way people feel and not necessarily the reality of truth. Just as today we often find our reactions differing from what they "ought" to be, so it was in Bible times.

Furthermore, we can understand these troubling psalms better if we remember what the New Testament tells us about the Old Testament: "These things . . . ," Pauls says, "were written down for our instruction" (1 Cor. 10:11). If we put ourselves in the place of the psalmist, we will see that the enemies he faces on the physical level correspond in remarkable ways to the enemies we face on the spiritual level. The New Testament tells us that "we are not contending against flesh and blood" (Eph. 6:12). We often *feel* that people are our enemies, but they are not. Our feelings would tell us to cry out against those who attack or oppress us, just as the writers of the psalms do; but in reality we know that our true enemies are the pressures of the evil one, the philosophies of the world and the attitudes of the flesh within. Remember Jesus said, "Not what goes into the mouth defiles a man, but what comes out of the mouth, this defiles a man. . . . For out of the heart come evil thoughts, murder, adultery, fornication, theft, false witness, slander" (Matt. 15:11,19).

Thus when we read Psalms today, when we read of imprecations against enemies, we must think of our own temptations toward covetousness, jealousy or pride and ambition. If we do this, the severe language of Psalms makes great sense, for we are taught in the New Testament that we must deal severely with these inward attitudes. They have no right to be honored in a Christian's life.

This is what Jesus tells us in the Sermon on the Mount: "If your right eye causes you to sin, pluck it out and throw it away. . . . If your right hand causes you to sin, cut it off and throw it away" (Matt. 5:29,30). Jesus does not mean to do this literally. He simply means we are to deal with temptation ruthlessly. So the ruthless psalms picture the way we must deal with the real enemies of the heart. And the doubting psalms are not expressions of truth, but of the way life looks to someone who is thinking only within the boundaries of birth and death.

Book I, Man's Awareness of His Need

If we follow the ancient Jewish practice of linking the five books of Psalms with the five books of the Pentateuch, we will find a key to understanding the special grouping of psalms. As Genesis in the Pentateuch describes man's awareness of his need for God and his inadequacy in himself, so the first book of Psalms—Psalms 1 to 42—in general expresses that same sense of need. It begins in Psalm 1 with a picture of the perfect man, just as Genesis begins with man in the Garden of Eden. Psalm 2 presents man in his rebellion: "Why are the nations in an uproar, and the peoples devising a vain thing? The kings of the earth take their stand, and the rulers take counsel together against the Lord and against His Anointed: Let us tear their fetters apart, and cast away their cords from us!" (vv. 1-3, *NASB*).

Psalms 3 through 7 are various expressions of man's sense of rejection and of attack from the world and enemies without. But Psalm 8 is a marvelous expression of man's awareness of an eternal destiny and a deep and intimate relationship which he once enjoyed with God and which he hopes will be restored. Even in his brokenness, man is learning to worship, and cries out: "O Lord, our Lord, how majestic is thy name in all the earth!"

Psalm 8 is paralleled in Psalm 19 which also reflects upon the glory of God in nature and compares it with the glory revealed through revelation. In these two psalms are expressed God's double method of communicating with His human family through the things He has made and the things He has said.

The fourteenth Psalm is a recognition of the folly of being ungodly and a reassurance to those who seek to walk with God: though the ungodly seem to flourish, a certain judgment will overtake them unless they repent. Psalm 16, along with Psalms 2, 22 and 40, are messianic psalms, clearly predicting the sufferings of Christ and the glory which should follow. Portions of these psalms are quoted in the New Testament and applied to the life of Jesus. Psalm 16 is particularly the psalm of resurrection, referred to as such by Peter on the Day of Pentecost where he quotes verse 10: "For Thou dost not give me up to Sheol, or let thy godly one see the pit" (see also Acts 2:27). Psalm 22 describes in a most remarkable way details of the crucifixion, beginning with the very words of Jesus from the cross, "My God, my God, why hast thou forsaken me?" Graphic details are given, even including the prophecy of the soldiers casting lots over Christ's seamless robe, and the piercing of Jesus' hands and feet.

The universal favorite of all the psalms is found in this section, Psalm 23. Here is the great Shepherd seeking the lost sheep and leading him into green pastures and beside still waters. Psalm 27 is a song of confidence in God's sovereign ability to strengthen the life and steady the heart in the face of conflict and distress. Psalms 28 through 31 describe various experiences of David and his recognition of his need for God's help in these circumstances. Psalm 32 is the noteworthy psalm of repentance and forgiveness. This psalm meant so much to Saint Augustine that he had it carved on wood and hung at the foot of his bed that he might see it every morning when he awoke. The apostle Paul quotes from it in Romans 4 as an example of what God will do with human sin when it is confessed before Him.

The closing psalms of Book I express the human heart's deep-seated longing in its separation from God and its desire to find Him in the midst of need. Psalm 40 is a beautiful example of this: "I waited patiently for the Lord; and He inclined to me, and heard my cry. He brought me up out of the pit of destruction, out of the miry clay; and He set my feet upon a rock making my footsteps firm. And He put a new song in my mouth, a song of praise to our God" (Ps. 40:1-3, *NASB*).

Psalm 41, which closes Book I, looks back to Psalm 1 and describes the blessed man—this time not one who is perfect in his own integrity, but one whom the Lord protects and sustains. This psalm ends the book with the doxology: "Blessed be the Lord, the God of Israel, from everlasting to everlasting! Amen and Amen" (v.13).

Book II, Man's Longing for Deliverance

The second book of psalms covers Psalms 42 through 72, and corresponds in theme to the book of Exodus. As Exodus tells us the story of Israel in captivity in Egypt— describing their sorrow, their bondage and the slavery of sin, yet learning much of the grace of God in His power to deliver them and bring them out of captivity—so the second book of psalms traces the same theme in a wider human experience. The slavery of sin and the longing for deliverance is beautifully expressed in the opening words of Psalm 42: "As the deer pants for the water brooks, so my soul pants for Thee, O God. My soul thirsts for God, for the living God; when shall I come and appear before God? My tears have been my food day and night, while they say to me all day long, 'Where is your God?' " (vv. 1-3, *NASB*).

But immediately the theme focuses upon the greatness of God and His power. Book II finds its theme in Psalm 45 which describes God as King, ruling in sovereignty over man and all his experiences. The book also closes with a psalm of the King, Psalm 72, in which God is pictured in mighty conquering power, setting man free from the bondage which has enslaved him.

Psalm 46 becomes a very appropriate expression of confidence in God as a refuge: "God is our refuge and strength, a very present help in trouble." Psalm 50 looks at God as the Judge of the earth, describing Him as: "The Mighty One, God the Lord, speaks and summons the earth from the rising of the sun to its setting. Out of Zion, the perfection of beauty, God shines forth. Our God comes, he does not keep silence, before him is devouring fire, round about him a mighty tempest" (vv. 1-3).

The theme of redemption is continued in Psalm 51, which is one of the great biblical expressions of confession and cleansing from sin. This was written after David's twin sins of murder and adultery, and records first his godly sorrow then his forthright confession and desire to turn from his evil, calling for the forgiveness of God and God's restoration to service so that he might tell others of the restoring grace of a loving God.

Psalm 59 includes a good example of the imprecations of God's people when they are suffering persecution and oppression: "My God in His lovingkindness will meet me; God will let me look triumphantly upon my foes. Do not slay them, lest my people forget; scatter them by Thy power, and bring them down, O Lord, our shield. On account of the sin of their mouth and the words of their lips, let them even be caught in their pride, and on account of curses and lies which they utter. Destroy them in wrath, destroy them, that they may be no more; that men may know that God rules in Jacob, to the ends of the earth" (vv. 10-13, *NASB*).

Many of us today feel exactly like this when we are being persecuted or oppressed, but we must always remember that the New Testament reveals that we do not wrestle against flesh and blood. Our oppressors are victims themselves and need our prayers and help that they may be delivered from that which causes them to act with cruelty and bitterness.

Psalms 60 through 64 describe similar experiences of repression. Psalm 65 breaks out into a note of praise for God's delivering grace. This theme is continued through

Psalms 66-68. But like Israel at the Red Sea, having been delivered from the bondage of Egypt and yet sinking again into despair at the waters before them, so Psalm 69 cries out: "Save me, O God! For the waters have come up to my neck. I sink in deep mire, where there is no foothold; I have come into deep waters, and the flood sweeps over me. I am weary with my crying; my throat is parched. My eyes grow dim with waiting for my God" (vv. 1-3). This beautiful psalm moves on to describe sufferings which could only have been fulfilled in the sufferings of Jesus, and several of the verses are quoted in the New Testament in this way.

But again deliverance comes from the mighty hand of God and, as we have already seen, the book closes with the great psalm of the King and the doxology: "Blessed be the Lord God, the God of Israel, who alone works wonders. And blessed be His glorious name forever; and may the whole earth be filled with His glory. Amen, and Amen" (Ps. 72:18,19, *NASB*).

Book III, Man's Heart Before God

Psalms 73 through 89 constitute the third book of Psalms. This corresponds in theme to the book of Leviticus which is the book of Tabernacle worship, the discovery of what God is like when man comes before Him and what man is like in the presence of God. Thus the theme of Book III reveals the inner workings of man's heart and his discovery of what God is like.

Psalm 73 opens the book by facing one of the most common problems of faith in an unbelieving world—the problem of why the ungodly prosper and seem to enjoy so much of God's blessing while the righteous suffer. The psalmist describes how terribly unfair this seemed to him until he went into the sanctuary and there learned what the end of the unrighteous will be. His conclusion is: "For, behold, those who are far from Thee will perish; Thou hast destroyed all those who are unfaithful to Thee. But as for me, the nearness of God is my good; I have made the Lord God my refuge, that I may tell of all Thy works" (73:27,28, *NASB*). This psalm establishes the theme of Book III. It describes the sanctuary of God in which truth is seen in all its reality.

This theme is continued through Psalm 78. These psalms lay heavy emphasis upon the duty of believers to look back upon God's dealings in the past and remember what they learned through their previous times of deliverance in order to help them in the present. Psalm 77 is a particularly vivid description of one who loses his sense of faith altogether and is only restored by thoughtful consideration of the unchangeable record of God's dealings in the past.

Psalms 80 and 81 describe the sense of wrongdoing which believers experience that they may learn to value afresh the forgiveness and restoration of God. Psalm 80 links with Psalm 23 as a further ministry of the great Shepherd of Israel to His believing flock.

A new theme is introduced in Psalms 81 through 84, depicting God's desire to be with His people, to see them delivered from their iniquities and to abundantly heap upon them blessings He desires to give. The beautiful eighty-fourth psalm which has been put to music and is frequently sung, is an expression of the New Testament emphasis upon the indwelling of God in the human heart. It is clear that Old Testament believers experienced this indwelling as fully as New Testament believers do, but they came to the knowledge of it by a more roundabout and shadowy method, for they were being taught by symbols and ceremonies rather than by direct statement of truth.

Again Psalms 85 through 88 record the psalmist's cry for God's deliverance; and the closing psalm of Book III, 89, is a magnificent description of God's covenant promise upon which the believer may safely rest. This psalm is a poetic counterpart to the covenant God made with David, described in 2 Samuel 7. The psalm goes on to speak prophetically of the culmination of the Davidic line in Jesus and the fullness of deliverance which He will bring. Beyond David is seen David's greater Son, and He is described in these words: "My faithfulness and My lovingkindness will be with him, and in My name his horn will be exalted. I shall also set his hand on the sea, and his right hand on the rivers. He will cry to Me, 'Thou art my Father, my God, and the rock of my salvation.' I also shall make him My first-born, the highest of the kings of the earth. My lovingkindness I will keep for him forever, and My covenant shall be confirmed to him" (vv. 24-28, *NASB*).

On this triumphant theme Book III closes with the briefest benediction: "Blessed be the Lord for ever! Amen and Amen."

Book IV, Man's Wilderness Experience

The book of Numbers is the record of the wanderings of the children of Israel in the wilderness for 40 years, so the fourth book of Psalms, covering Psalms 90 through 106, reflects the up and down wilderness experience of a believer. This alternating theme is clearly seen in Psalms 90 and 91. Psalm 90 was written by Moses and was undoubtedly sung by Israel during the days of their wilderness wanderings. It is a recognition of the frailty of men and the justice and greatness of God. The psalmist describes life thus: "For all our days have declined in Thy fury; we have finished our years like a sigh. As for the days of our life, they contain seventy years, or if due to strength, eighty years, yet their pride is but labor and sorrow; for soon it is gone and we fly away" (vv. 9,10, *NASB*).

Yet the next psalm, 91, is the very opposite. It describes the delight of one who has turned to the Lord and dwells in the secret shelter of the Most High. When the believer walks closely with his God, even in the wilderness, his heart is kept strong and confident, but when he wanders away, trusting in his own resources, he feels estranged from God and suffers under a sense of guilt and condemnation. The alternating experience is seen again in Psalm 95 which opens with the familiar words: "O come, let us sing for joy to the Lord; let us shout joyfully to the rock of our salvation. Let us come before His presence with thanksgiving; let us shout joyfully to Him with psalms" (vv. 1,2, *NASB*).

Yet in verse 8 the voice of God is heard: "Do not harden your hearts, as at Meribah, as in the day of Massah in the wilderness; when your fathers tested Me, they tried Me, though they had seen My work. For forty years I loathed that generation, and said they are a people who err in their heart, and they do not know My ways" (*NASB*).

Psalms 96 through 101 are all psalms of rejoicing, but in Psalm 102 the psalmist bewails his aimless existence and says: "My days are like a lengthened shadow; and I wither away like grass" (v. 11, *NASB*). The closing verses of this psalm are quoted in Hebrews 1 as referring to Jesus: "Thou, Lord, in the beginning didst lay the foundation of the earth; and the heavens are the works of Thy hands; they will perish, but Thou remainest; and they all will become old as a garment, and as a mantle Thou wilt roll them up; as a garment they will also be changed. But Thou art the same, and Thy years will not come to an end" (Heb. 1:10-12, *NASB*).

Thus even in the wilderness experiences of life there is a continual recognition of the presence of One who will not forsake; One who never relaxes His vigilance even though those whom He guards are unaware of His presence. The apostle Paul in 1 Corinthians 10:4 says that the Israelites "were drinking from a spiritual rock which followed them; and the rock was Christ" (*NASB*).

Psalms 103 through 106 are historic psalms, reviewing Israel's past experiences of deliverance by the hand of the Lord in order that the faith of God's people might be awakened in the present and they will be encouraged to endure their present trials. Book IV, therefore, appropriately closes with the cry: "Save us, O Lord our God, and gather us from among the nations, to give thanks to Thy holy name and glory in Thy praise" (106:47, *NASB*).

Book V, Man's Deliverance

The fifth and longest book of Psalms corresponds to the book of Deuteronomy in theme. It records the fullness of deliverance brought about by the resources of God instead of by reliance upon dedicated human resources. Psalm 107 introduces this theme with a remarkable sequence of deliverances, all achieved by men in various circumstances who cry to the Lord in their troubles and find that He is able to deliver them. The experiences cited correspond remarkably with various attitudes and depressions which believers experience today. There are those who seem to wander in desert places. There are those who sit as prisoners held in bonds of iron and affliction. There are those who are sick because of their sinful ways and who spend their days in jaded and restless boredom. There are those who face great danger and pressure and yet in it all they find God adequate to deliver when they abandon trust in their own resources.

Psalm 109 is regarded as the most severe of the imprecatory psalms, but certain indications suggest that the imprecations are properly viewed as quotations from the psalmist's enemies and represent the things they are saying about him. Viewed in that sense the psalm is another great expression of the power of God to sustain under bitter attack. Psalms 110 and 118 are clearly messianic psalms, looking beyond David's experience to a completer fulfillment in Jesus and His universal reign.

Psalm 119 is the longest psalm in the book of Psalms and follows the Hebrew alphabet with 22 sections, each of which begins with a different alphabet letter. The theme of Psalm 119 is the Word of God and its remarkable power to examine the heart and deal with the thoughts and intents of man's inner life, correct and sustain the spirit, and in every way accomplish the work and will of God.

Psalms 120 through 134 are called Songs of Ascent, and were sung by worshipers as they marched up to Jerusalem from various parts of the land to offer their sacrifices in the Temple. They contain beautiful expressions of thanksgiving and praise to God as the deliverer and protector of His people.

Psalm 137 seems to be the one psalm which comes out of the exile of Israel in Babylon. It is probably the last of the psalms written and was added to the collection probably by Ezra the priest. Psalm 139 corresponds in theme to Psalm 8, and recognizes the omniscience and omnipresence of God in relationship to a single individual, and God's knowledge of the human makeup. A short section of the psalms, from 140 through 143, reflect various prayers for God's help; but beginning with Psalm 144 to Psalm 150 there is almost unbroken praise and thanksgiving, expressed in magnificent language. These psalms sound one triumphant note all through, and the closing psalm is made up of hallelujah: "Praise the Lord."

These triumphant psalms are the expression of someone so excited about God that all he can do is shout "Hallelujah!" That will always be the experience of one who learns to understand the pattern of God's working in his life.

The psalms are designed to teach us to do one primary thing—to worship. Though they reflect every human emotion, they do so in a distinct and important way: They are emotions seen in relationship to God. Every psalm is written as in the very presence of God. This book there-fore teaches us how to be honest before God. If you have a problem in your life, tell God about it. Don't hide it. Don't cover it up. Especially, do not become pious and sanctimonious and try to act as though there is no trouble. If you feel angry with God, it is best to say so. If you are upset about something, tell Him your sense of disturbance but remind Him also that you know how foolish it is to be upset with Him. If you are resentful, bring that out. If you are happy and joyful, express that. This is what worship is—a heart pouring out honest reactions to a God who can both correct and restore. If we learn to be honest before God even about troubles and problems, wrong moods and resentful attitudes, we shall quickly find His grace answering our needs.

CHAPTER THREE

The Searchings of Mind and Will

PROVERBS

In ordinary everyday conversation we frequently describe the functions of our personality as mind, emotions and will, but Scripture does not follow this order; it would put them emotions, will and mind. As we have already seen, the book of Psalms is the expression of our human emotions. In similar manner the book of Proverbs is the expression of the will, while Ecclesiastes is the record of the investigations of the mind. Proverbs, therefore, sets before us the choices of life. Those choices govern all that we do and say and are therefore the very heart of our conscious existence. Both the emotions and reason are to be considered in making up our minds, but the final decision of the will governs our conduct and ultimate destiny.

The profound significance of these choices is beautifully described in the introduction to the book of Proverbs: "The proverbs of Solomon the son of David, king of Israel: to know wisdom and instruction, to discern the sayings of understanding, to receive instruction in wise behavior, righteousness, justice and equity; to give prudence to the naive, to the youth knowledge and discretion, a wise man will hear and increase in learning, and a man of understanding will acquire wise counsel, to understand a proverb and a figure, the words of the wise, and their riddles" (Prov. 1:1-6, *NASB*).

Proverbs is the book designed expressly to help us confront the mysteries of life. It covers the whole of life, from childhood through youth and maturity, and gives us very practical guidance for very practical problems.

As the introduction suggests, most of the book comes from the pen of Solomon, the son of David and the wisest king Israel ever had. When young Solomon succeeded his father as king of Israel, he was granted a vision from God in which he was permitted to choose what his heart desired above everything else. Solomon asked that he be granted wisdom to fit him for the task of ruling. Because he asked for this instead of riches or fame, God gave him all three. The book consists, then, of the laws of heaven applied in a logical and reasonable way to life on earth. The secret of it is given in verse 7, chapter 1: "The fear of the Lord is the beginning of knowledge; fools despise wisdom and instruction."

The fear of the Lord mentioned here is not a craven fear that God is going to whip or torment us, but rather a fear that we might hurt His loving heart and awaken His just correction toward us. The closest English translation is really "reverence" or "respect." In a world of deceit and illusion, the greatest gift we can be given is the gift of truth. We are told at the beginning of this book that God is the source of truth and the only trustworthy source; therefore the fear of the Lord is the beginning of knowledge of the truth. It is not the end; it is but the beginning. And only the one who in his heart has a continuing respect for God's wisdom can properly evaluate and understand life.

The book appears to be difficult to outline, as, like the dictionary, it seems to change the subject with every verse. But there is a definite structure which can be detected. Following the brief introduction there is a series

of ten remarkable discourses on wisdom which are the
wise teachings of a father to his son. Ten times in the first
nine chapters we find words to this effect: "Hear, my son
. . ." These discourses begin with the child in the home
and then follow the youth as he moves out into the busy
streets of the city and encounters various new circumstances of life. He is taught how to choose and make
friends, how to face the perils which are at work to destroy
his life, and finally to discover the forces which will make
him strong.

These "facts of life" discourses are followed by two
collections of proverbs—from chapter 10 through 24 and
from chapter 25 through chapter 31. The collection in
chapters 25 to 29 is said to be "the proverbs of Solomon
which the men of Hezekiah king of Judah copied" (25:1)
some centuries after Solomon's death. The closing two
chapters bring before us the words of two otherwise
unknown individuals; Agur, son of Jakeh, in chapter 30
and Lemuel, king of Massa, whose words are found in
chapter 31.

Concerning the Choosing of One's Friends

Chapters 1 and 2 are given largely to the problem of
how to choose one's friends while yet young in years.
Perhaps nothing is more important for a child to learn
early in life, for the influence of peers has a powerful
effect. Two types of friends are described, personified as
two alluring women who cry to us from the streets of the
city and the public places of life. One reflects the divine
view of life which is true reality. The other is described as
a "loose woman" whose smooth words reflect the popular
outlook of the day; and though they sound fair and logical
they lead to ruin and death. Confronted by these two
contrary outlooks the young believer is exhorted. "My
son, if you will receive my sayings, and treasure my
commandments within you, make your ear attentive to

wisdom, incline your heart to understanding; for if you cry for discernment, lift your voice for understanding; if you seek her as silver and search for her as for hidden treasures; then you will discern the fear of the Lord, and discover the knowledge of God. For the Lord gives wisdom; from His mouth come knowledge and understanding" (2:1-6, *NASB*).

Chapter 3 follows the young man as he grows up and makes his way into the city and is immediately confronted with pressures and temptations. The section speaks very delicately and frankly about the pressures of sex and about the destruction that wrong responses to these pressures can effect on a life. There is also strong admonition against getting involved in shady financial transactions.

No young person ever imagines that he or she will become a failure in life. No one has ever said to me, "My ambition is to be a bum on skid row." Yet the heartbreak of life is that with the best of intentions, and often with frightening rapidity, we can suddenly find ourselves in trouble up to our ears and all our dreams of glory faded and gone. A young man recently told me of how he had left his home and moved to the city and did what he thought was right and what he hoped would fulfill him. At the urging of new friends he became involved in drugs until he began to experiment with LSD and ended up mainlining on heroin, experiencing fantastic hallucinations. He eventually became a procurer for a prostitute on the streets of San Francisco and there, like the prodigal son, he finally awakened to what was happening to him and began to seek God again.

That is the kind of thing that the writer of Proverbs is seeking to forestall. He points out that life is simply too big for us to handle by ourselves. No matter how good advice may seem to be, if it is not consistent with what God has told us, it is not to be trusted. Thus he sums up the section by saying: "Trust in the Lord with all your heart,

and do not rely on your own insight. In all your ways
acknowledge him, and he will make straight your paths.
Be not wise in your own eyes; fear the Lord, and turn
away from evil. It will be healing to your flesh and
refreshment to your bones" (3:5-8).

Once again the two ways of life are symbolized by two
women. One is an adventuress, bold and impudent, offering immediate pleasure and delights but actually intent
only on self-satisfaction. Whoever follows this philosophy is like an ox led to the slaughter or a stag or bird
caught by a hunter. In chapter 7 the young believer is
warned: "Do not let your heart turn aside to her ways, do
not stray into her paths. For many are the victims she has
cast down, and numerous are all her slain. Her house is
the way to Sheol, descending to the chambers of death"
(vv. 25-27, *NASB*). It is not merely sexual sins which are
thus described, but the whole philosophy of the world
which offers fame and fulfillment and suggests that we
deserve the very best and finest things of life. One only
has to listen to the commericals on television or view the
advertisements in magazines to see the same philosophy
abounding today.

But in chapters 8 and 9 the delights of true wisdom are
described. Here are the secrets hidden (from the natural
man) from the very foundations of the earth which touch
upon the deep things of life and reveal the true secrets of
security and true identity. This all corresponds exactly
with the advice of the apostle Paul in Romans 12:2: "Do
not be conformed to this world, but be transformed by the
renewal of your mind, that you may prove what is the will
of God, what is good and acceptable and perfect."

Concerning Most of Life's Situations
Beginning with chapter 10 through chapter 24 are the
actual proverbs of Solomon; all very pithy, practical
words of advice concerning most of the situations of life.

The method of teaching is either by contrast or by climax. In the contrast the writer sets two things side by side and shows the good and evil results of various attitudes and actions. In the teaching by climax he makes a statement in the first half which is then enlarged upon and concluded in the second. A vivid example of contrast is found in 10:7: "The memory of the righteous is a blessing, but the name of the wicked will rot." Another is found in 10:10: "He who winks the eye causes trouble, but he who boldly reproves makes peace." There the deceitful look expressed by a wink is contrasted with the one who frankly and forthrightly speaks truth, even though what he says is not especially welcome. The result of that kind of frankness is peace.

An example of climax is found in 10:22: "The blessing of the Lord makes rich, and he adds no sorrow with it." Again in 11:31: "If the righteous is requited on earth, how much more the wicked and the sinner!"

Another form of teaching is that of vivid simile, such as 10:26: "Like vinegar to the teeth, and smoke to the eyes, so is the sluggard to those who send him." As vinegar sets the teeth on edge and smoke burns the eyes, so is the man who is entrusted with a message but who dawdles along the way. Another of this sort is found in 11:22: "Like a gold ring in a swine's snout is a beautiful woman without discretion." Imagine an ugly pig with swill dripping from its mouth, but with a gold ring affixed to its nostril! The gold ring signifies value, but it is in the wrong place. So is a beautiful woman who has not learned that true beauty is the inner beauty of spirit.

Still another of this type is found in 12:4: "A good wife is the crown of her husband, but she who brings shame is like rottenness in his bones."

These observations clearly reflect a true evaluation of life rather than the shallow and artificial viewpoints found in the world's thinking.

The chapters of Proverbs cover a wide range of subjects and do so in short, pithy epigrams; but there are also more extended treatments of subjects. For instance in chapter 12:16-22 there is a short discourse on the tongue and the dangers and blessings which can come from it: "A fool's vexation is known at once, but a prudent man conceals dishonor. He who speaks truth tells what is right, but a false witness, deceit. There is one who speaks rashly like the thrusts of a sword, but the tongue of the wise brings healing. Truthful lips will be established forever, but a lying tongue is only for a moment. Deceit is in the heart of those who devise evil, but counselors of peace have joy. No harm befalls the righteous, but the wicked are filled with trouble. Lying lips are an abomination to the Lord, but those who deal faithfully are His delight" (*NASB*).

There is not only truth for young people in Proverbs, but also wisdom for parents. In 13:24 there is a verse which many children have wished were not included in the Scriptures: "He who spares the rod hates his son, but he who loves him is diligent to discipline him." This is the biblical basis for the saying: "This hurts me more than it does you!" In this connection also 22:6 is an often quoted verse: "Train up a child in the way he should go, and when he is old he will not depart from it." The first part of this verse should really be translated "Train up a child according to his way." This means a parent should find out what is in the child and bring him up according to his natural bent, so that what God has hidden in him may be developed and drawn out. A child trained in these ways will not depart from that training when he is older.

Further wisdom concerning discipline is found in 23:13,14: "Do not withhold discipline from a child; if you beat him with a rod, he will not die. If you beat him with the rod you will save his life from Sheol." The rod here is not an iron rod or even a thick stick, but a light twig which stings but does not bruise. This is of course counsel for parents with small children. When dealing with adolescents it is quite different.

Certain of the Proverbs present very profound insights into the nature of life and reality. It would be good to commit them to memory since they represent a necessary understanding of life. One such is found in 14:12: "There is a way which seems right to a man, but its end is the way to death." How clearly this states that our own actions nearly always seem right in our own eyes, but we cannot see the end. Here again we must not rely upon our own judgment but trust in the wisdom of God.

Another verse of profound insight is 20:27: "The spirit of man is the lamp of the Lord, searching all his innermost parts." This is probably one of the most important verses in the Bible to help us properly understand our humanity. Our human spirits are designated the "lamp of the Lord" and this is true whether the individual is a believer or an unbeliever. But the "lamp" is not a light. The human spirit is the lampstand, made and designed to project a light, but the light itself is that of the Holy Spirit of God. When the lamp of the spirit holds the light of the Holy Spirit, then one is enabled to search the innermost part of one's life and to understand oneself for the first time. Where the lamp does not hold the light of God, the individual dwells in darkness and walks and lives in darkness.

Still another insight into human nature is found in 19:3: "When a man's folly brings his way to ruin, his heart rages against the Lord." How true to life this is! When someone's foolishness brings him into trouble, whom does he blame? The Lord, of course, or if he is married perhaps he takes it like a man and blames it on his wife, as Adam did in the Garden of Eden. But the ultimate blame is cast upon the Lord.

This should lead one to say in the words of 20:9: "Who can say, 'I have made my heart clean; I am pure from my sin'?" An honest answer to that question will soon put the blame for evil where it properly belongs and open the way for the cleansing of God.

Concerning What God Has Concealed

In chapter 25 begins the second collection of proverbs which were copied by the men of Hezekiah. Verse 2 is very suggestive in this connection: "It is the glory of God to conceal things, but the glory of kings is to search things out." This suggests a possible reason why King Hezekiah set his men to copy the proverbs of Solomon which had not previously been recorded, for he was a king who loved to search out what God had hidden. If you want to have a royal experience, I suggest that you search the Word of God for the things God has concealed there. You will find it an exciting treasure hunt and highly rewarding.

Chapter 26 has some very helpful words about troublesome people in general. Verses 3-12 present a series on fools and how to handle them. Verses 13-16 tell us what to do about sluggards and what is wrong with laziness. Verses 17-23 concern meddlers and how to handle them. Then verse 24 to the chapter's end is all about the loveless—those who hate others. Here we learn what hatred will do to the man who indulges in it.

These proverbs from the men of Hezekiah reflect the concern of rulers and kings for the rights of their people. For instance, in 28:27 we are told: "He who gives to the poor will not want, but he who hides his eyes will get many a curse." Again in 29:7: "A righteous man knows the rights of the poor; a wicked man does not understand such knowledge." Still again in 29:14: "If a king judges the poor with equity his throne will be established for ever." These proverbs clearly recognize the problem caused by social injustice and lay the responsibility to correct this not only upon the king but on individual citizens in the realm as well. We must ever remember, "no man is an island." We must not shut ourselves away from those around us who are less fortunate than we. These proverbs remind us that we have a responsibility toward them.

Chapter 30 contains the words of Agur. This chapter somewhat parallels the closing chapters of Job, for Agur is greatly impressed by the wisdom of God in nature and His power and might as contrasted with the frailty of human beings. He finds numerous examples in nature which give warnings against disobedience toward parents, to excite the imagination and awaken wonder, to warn against allowing sudden good fortune to go to one's head, and to encourage those who feel very small and insignificant yet do great and remarkable things.

When Agur says: "Three things . . .; four" (see vv. 15,18,21,29) he is not being uncertain as to the number but is using this climactic formula as a way of emphasizing the truth he presents.

Chapter 31 contains the words of Lemuel, king of Massa. We know nothing more about him, but in a brief section he is given certain exhortations about royal responsibilities and the chapter concludes with a most remarkable poem in acrostic form (each verse begins with a new letter of the Hebrew alphabet), which seems also to come from the pen of Lemuel. It praises the model wife who is devoted to her husband's and children's welfare and interests and is diligent and tireless in providing for all her family's needs. She is gracious toward those outside the family and amply deserves the gratitude of her husband and children.

The secret of her accomplishment is given in verse 30: "A woman who fears the Lord is to be praised." It is remarkable that in this description of the model wife the woman is involved in much work that would often be thought of as "man's" labor. She buys and plants fields, she sells goods which she herself manufactures and she works beside her husband in all the enterprises of life. There is only one field which she does not enter, and that is the realm of government. It is her husband who sits in the gates among the elders of the land. The participation of women in government was not unknown in Israel, as witness Deborah the judge, and Hannah the prophetess. But these served not as men but in their unique function as women, supporting and augmenting the male leaders.

The nature of Proverbs is such that it requires frequent reading to absorb its content. Dr. Billy Graham has made a habit of reading Proverbs through once a month. This is made easier by the fact that the book has 31 chapters corresponding with the number of days in most months. The book is so filled with practical, earthy wisdom that it would not be too much to read a chapter of Proverbs every day of a lifetime. Undoubtedly it would save from many heartaches and introduce many blessings.

ECCLESIASTES

The book of Ecclesiastes is unique in the Bible, for there is no other book which limits itself to a completely human rather than a divine point of view. As a consequence, the book of Ecclesiastes contains error, and yet it is wholly inspired. This may confuse some because many feel that inspiration is the guarantee of truth; but this is not necessarily so. Inspiration merely guarantees accuracy of a particular point of view. If it is God's point of view the statement is completely true. If it is man's point of view, or even the devil's point of view, it may be true or it may not be true. Only careful comparison with the divine point of view will determine which it is.

This is what makes possible the charge that one can prove all kinds of things by quoting the Bible. This is certainly true; but what is often being ignored is that the Bible invariably points out the error and makes it clear that it is error. In the opening two verses of this book, it is carefully pointed out that what is recorded is not divine truth. In verse 2 and many times throughout the course of the book the phrase "under the sun" is repeated. Everything in the book is evaluated according to outward appearance—that is, man's point of view of reality. It is only that which can be observed under the sun.

It is this character that makes the book of Ecclesiastes the favorite book of atheists and agnostics. Many of the cults quote frequently from this book, because it gives purely naturalistic views of death and immortality. For instance in 3:18-20 it says: "I said to myself concerning the sons of men, 'God has surely tested them in order for them to see that they are but beasts.' For the fate of the sons of men and the fate of beasts is the same. As one dies so dies the other; indeed, they all have the same breath and there is no advantage for man over beast, for all is vanity. All go to the same place. All came from the dust and all return to the dust" (*NASB*). Clearly this is a contradiction of what is taught elsewhere in the Bible, that man is different from the beasts, and that beyond man's physical death lies a continuing existence with awareness and personal expression. Yet only divine revelation can teach us that truth. Man's observation "under the sun" makes it appear that man is no different from the beasts and his death no different from theirs.

Ecclesiastes, however, is not an atheistic book, for to be atheistic is to be unrealistic and the Bible is never unrealistic. Atheists are those who have convinced themselves, by somewhat tortured argument, that there is no God, though every inward testimony of their conscience and the structure of the universe around give constant witness to the fact that there is a God. Usually it takes a good deal of education to be an atheist, and it is a remarkable fact that primitive people are never atheistic. Atheism arises from a desire to escape life's reality, and especially a desire to escape any sense of responsibility toward a God to whom one must answer. But Ecclesiastes is not atheistic, even though it is written from a humanistic point of view. Ecclesiastes views God as men in general view God: as waiting at the end of life to subject men to judgment and possible condemnation, but not offering anything vital to the enjoyment of life during the life span.

Though the name of Solomon is never mentioned in the book, the writer identifies himself in the very first verse as the son of David, king in Jerusalem. Even some evangelical scholars have felt that certain indications in the book require a writer who lived much later than Solomon's time. It may be possible that some of the words of Solomon were incorporated into a work written some time after Solomon's reign. However, King Solomon was in an unusual position to undertake the experiments and investigations reflected in this book, for during the 40 years of his reign there was utter peace in the kingdom of Judah and Israel. Since he did not have to concern himself with military pursuits, he had all the time he needed to follow through with investigations into the meaning of life. Furthermore, he had all the wealth he needed and was possessed with a keen, logical and discerning mind which had gained for him the reputation as the wisest man in the world.

The value of Ecclesiastes, therefore, is that it sets forth life from the standpoint of the natural man apart from divine revelation and views life from the best possible advantage.

In most of our modern versions, the writer calls himself "the Preacher." This, however, is not a good translation of the Hebrew word used. The idea is one who investigates or gathers facts together; perhaps the best translation would be "the Searcher." The book presents the conclusions of one whose brilliant mind has searched through all the phenomena of life and come up with one definite conclusion. That conclusion is stated in verse 2: "Vanity of vanities, says the Preacher, vanity of vanities! All is vanity. " We use the word *vanity* in a different sense today. To us vanity is conceit over personal appearance. If someone spends long hours primping before a mirror we regard him/her as suffering from personal vanity. But in Ecclesiastes vanity means emptiness, futility, meaninglessness. When the Searcher has completed his survey of life he says that everything is futile and without meaning—there is no sense to anything.

He supports this conclusion with a series of arguments gleaned from sifting through various philosophies of life. Perhaps the most interesting thing about this book is that all the philosophies by which men have attempted to live are summarized here. To quote from the book: "There is nothing new under the sun." Though we are almost 30 centuries removed from the time of the writing of this book, yet nothing new has been produced in the world of ideas than what is reflected here.

The Searcher first investigates what might be described as *the scientific outlook,* or the mechanistic view of the universe. His view of nature is that it is a meaningless cycle of processes which repeat themselves without progress or meaning. His conclusion is: "That which has been is that which will be, and that which has been done is that which will be done. So, there is nothing new under the sun" (1:9, *NASB*). Nevertheless, there are some remarkable recognitions of the scientific processes here which were not known in the world of science of Solomon's day. For instance, there is a description of the circuit of the winds, "The wind blows to the south, and goes round to the north; round and round goes the wind, and on its circuits the wind returns" (1:6). Men of science were not aware of this until some centuries after this book was written. There is also a description of the evaporation cycle of circulating waters: "All streams run to the sea, but the sea is not full; to the place where the streams flow, there they flow again" (1:7). Though the writer has this keen insight into nature, his outlook is that life goes on and we are lost in the meaninglessness of the universe where nothing is to be heard but the clanking of gears. This is a very common philosophy today. What is man in a universe like this? He is but a tiny speck with no meaning or significance whatever.

In chapter 2 the writer examines *the philosophy of hedonism*—the pursuit of pleasure as the chief end of life. What will give life meaning? Millions today say: "Just enjoy yourself. Have a good time. Live life with gusto. Do as you like. Seek pleasure. That is the purpose of living. That's why we are here." So the Searcher says: "I said to myself, 'Come now, I will make a test of pleasure; enjoy yourself.' But behold, this also was vanity" (2:1). Then he proceeds to itemize the pleasures he sought. He first tried pleasure in the form of laughter or mirth. He sought out opportunities to give himself to genial, laughing, happy company; but after a time he says even this yielded weariness of spirit.

Then he tried acquisition of possessions. Perhaps meaning would come from wealth: "Then I became great and increased more than all who preceded me in Jerusalem. My wisdom also stood by me. And all that my eyes desired I did not refuse them. I did not withhold my heart from any pleasure, for my heart was pleased because of all my labor and this was my reward for all my labor" (2:9,10, *NASB*). But this too produced emptiness of spirit and did not satisfy his longings.

Then he says: "I turned to consider wisdom and madness and folly" that is, he set himself to investigate opposites in the realm of ideas. Though he saw that wisdom excels folly as light excels darkness, nevertheless his ultimate conclusion was that it all comes out at the same place. "Then I said to myself, 'As is the fate of the fool, it will also befall me. Why then have I been extremely wise?' So I said to myself, 'This too is vanity.' For there is no lasting remembrance of the wise man as with the fool, inasmuch as in the coming days all will be forgotten. And how the wise man and the fool alike die!" (2:15,16, *NASB*).

Then he comes to this terrible conclusion: "So I hated life, for the work which had been done under the sun was grievous to me; because everything is futility and striving after wind" (2:17, *NASB*).

Here is a man who has given himself to pleasure, to amassing possessions, to the pursuit of wisdom and the realm of ideas, and yet all he can say is: "I hated life." Despair is the end of it all.

Chapter 3 begins a second major discourse which ends at Ecclesiastes 5:20. It is an investigation of *what is called existentialism today*. Americans, I think, have difficulty understanding why existential thinking has so powerfully gripped the minds of people in our world. The philosophy became popular at the end of World War II when Europe was left in shambles and the great cities of Europe were in ruins. It was evident that all that men had previously pinned their hopes on—government and religion as they knew them—had been powerless to arrest the catastrophe and terrible chaos of World War II. At the end of it, men were left with utterly shattered hopes concerning what they had previously trusted in. They said to one another: "What can we trust? We can't trust religion, for it did nothing to stem the awful tide of tyranny under Hitler. We can't trust government because it is the very tool of such power. So what can we trust?"

Someone then suggested that the only thing to be trusted is one's own reactions to life as we experience various circumstances. Though no two persons may have the same reactions, at least each person's reaction is real to him. So the philosophy of existentialism became widespread.

Now the Searcher says: "I too tried this. I discovered that I also reacted to events and had certain inescapable experiences in life." He says: "For everything there is a season, and a time for every matter under heaven:

a time to be born, and a time to die;
a time to plant, and a time to pluck up what is planted;
a time to kill, and a time to heal;
a time to break down, and a time to build up;
a time to weep, and a time to laugh;
a time to mourn, and a time to dance;
a time to cast away stones, a time to gather stones together;
a time to embrace, and a time to refrain from embracing;
a time to seek, and a time to lose;
a time to keep, and a time to cast away;
a time to rend, and a time to sew;
a time to keep silence, and a time to speak;
a time to love, and a time to hate;
a time for war, and a time for peace.

"What gain has the worker from his toil?

"I have seen the business that God has given to the sons of men to be busy with. He has made everything beautiful in its time; also he has put eternity into man's mind, yet so that he cannot find out what God has done from the beginning to the end" (3:1-11).

Here is the explanation for all the restlessness of humanity. Man can never be content with simple existence. He must look deeper. Eternity is in his heart (see v. 11, *NASB*). So the events of life are inescapable and are experienced by all men, yet when they are over they all turn to dust; and despite the variety of experience man has not found contentment for there is a restless longing placed within him for something deeper. His conclusion, therefore, is: "There is nothing better for them than to be happy and enjoy themselves as long as they live" (3:12). This theme of "eat, drink and be merry for tomorrow we die" is repeated again and again throughout this book as the only workable relief to the endless discontent of life.

In chapter 4 the Searcher investigates what *we would call the "competitive enterprise" of life—capitalism.* When the Searcher tried the competitive system he saw that it resulted in injustices and oppression. Behind it were selfish motivations resulting in inequities. So he said it all came to the same end: "A poor, yet wise lad is better than an old and foolish king who no longer knows how to receive instruction" (4:13, *NASB*). In other words, what good does it do to get to the top of the heap when a young man at the bottom with nothing but a few smart ideas can surge ahead? What is the good of it all?

In chapter 5 *he tries religion,* to do good and to be good. Yet he points out that religious people can do very unethical things and they also oppress the poor. Furthermore, there is no power in deadly religious formalism to arrest wrongs or change inequities. So it too comes to the same end—emptiness and vanity.

Chapter 6 sets forth *his experiments with materialism*—the philosophy of the "good life." Once again he concludes: "If a man fathers a hundred children and lives many years, however many they be, but his soul is not satisfied with good things, and he does not even have a proper burial, then I say, 'Better the miscarriage than he' " (6:3, *NASB*). Thus if one has everything and yet there is still a craving which these things cannot satisfy, one is no better off than if he had never been born. It all comes to the same place.

In chapter 7, Solomon approaches life from *the standpoint of stoicism*—a cultivated indifference to events. In this philosophy there is an attempt to be moderate in all things, so the Searcher says: "I have seen everything during my lifetime of futility; there is a righteous man who perishes in his righteousness, and there is a wicked man who prolongs his life in his wickedness. Do not be excessively righteous, and do not be overly wise. Why should you ruin yourself? Do not be excessively wicked, and do not be a fool. Why should you die before your time?" (7:15-17, *NASB*).

Chapter 8 through the first eight verses of chapter 11 are a connected discourse examining what might be referred to as *the "common sense view" of life*. Anyone approaching life is exhorted to master the power structures of the world in which he lives. The Searcher says in effect, "Try to understand who is the boss and who is not and do your best to be on the right side at the right time." It is easy to recognize that philosophy around us today. But here is the Searcher's conclusion: "I saw every work of God, [and] I concluded that man cannot discover the work which has been done under the sun. Even though man should seek laboriously, he will not discover; and though the wise man should say, 'I know,' he cannot discover" (8:17, *NASB*).

Chapter 9 examines the world's value judgments which have an aura of wisdom about them but are not accurate. The race is not always to the swift or riches to the intelligent. The battle does not always go to the strong, for the Searcher says: "Moreover, man does not know his time: like fish caught in a treacherous net, and birds trapped in a snare, so the sons of men are ensnared at an evil time when it suddenly falls on them" (9:12, *NASB*).

Chapter 10 presents a collection of proverbs which exhort one to maintain discretion in life, but it is all an enlightened expression of selfishness which is the underlying motivation.

In chapter 11 success is seen as simply a matter of diligence. One need only work and apply himself. But then the Searcher concludes: "Indeed, if a man should live many years, let him rejoice in them all, and let him remember the days of darkness, for they shall be many. Everything that is to come will be futility" (11:8, *NASB*). So he has proved his case. All the way through it is the same: life lived from a human point of view comes out to meaninglessness and futility.

There comes a remarkable change of viewpoint at 11:9 and through the concluding chapter (chap. 12). All the way through the Searcher's investigation of life his continually repeated conclusion has been *"Eat drink and be merry, for tomorrow you must die."* It is stated in various ways in 2:24, 3:22, 5:18, 8:15, 9:7, and in 10:19 the Searcher says: "Bread is made for laughter, and wine gladdens life, and money answers everything." One has only to look around in modern life today to see that the world comes to the identical conclusion. It is the inevitable conclusion of any approach to life that erases God from the picture. Man is told to live like an animal, but this denies the glory of humanity. It reduces man to the level of the beast and the statement, "eat, drink and be merry" becomes the most hopeless statement one can make about life. What is life if it consists only of that? It is indeed utterly insignificant and without meaning. Life goes out like a candle flame in the end, and utter pessimism rules the life lived without God.

But the Searcher now speaks directly to youth and says: "Rejoice, young man, during your childhood, and let your heart be pleasant during the days of young manhood. And follow the impulses of your heart and the desires of your eyes. Yet know that God will bring you to judgment for all these things" (11:9, *NASB*).

Then a new, truer view is presented in 12:1: "Remember also your Creator in the days of your youth, before the evil days come, and the years draw nigh, when you will say, 'I have no pleasure in them' " (12:1). Verses 2 through 7 are a marvelously beautiful description of old age and death: ". . . the silver cord is snapped . . . the golden bowl is broken . . . the pitcher is broken at the fountain . . . the wheel broken at the cistern, and the dust returns to the earth as it was, and the spirit returns to God who gave it." Before this occurs, the Searcher says, youth are well-advised to put their lives in the hands of a loving Creator and to walk with Him through the varied experiences of life.

Thus a gleam of light comes at the end of this pessimistic book, for the Searcher concludes: "The end of the matter; all has been heard. Fear God, and keep his commandments; for this is the whole duty of man" (12:13). It is most unfortunate that the word "duty" has been inserted in this version, as well as others, for it is not in the Hebrew text. What the verse actually says is: "Fear God, and keep His commandments; for this is the wholeness of man." This is what makes man whole! The secret is to enthrone God in the days of your youth. If you want to find the secret of living so that the heart is satisfied and the spirit enriched and fulfilled according to God's intention, then "remember your Creator in the days of your youth, before the evil days come." Enthrone God at the center of your life and you will discover all that God intended life to be. You will be able to rejoice all the days of your life.

The philosophy that begins and ends in the dust and says that dust is all there is to life is indeed "vanity," utter folly. But the Searcher's ultimate conclusion is that wholeness comes from putting God at the center of life.

CHAPTER FOUR

The Urges of Love

SONG OF SOLOMON

Love songs are always popular, and this one is called in the Hebrew "The Song of Songs," which is a Hebrew expression for the best or finest of all. It is the last of the five books of poetry in the Old Testament. Job was the first; then Psalms, Proverbs and Ecclesiastes form a trilogy; the last is the Song of Solomon. As we have seen, these books reveal the basic elements of humanity. The most profound of the five is Job which represents the voice of the spirit in man, the deepest part of our nature. The trilogy of Psalms, Proverbs and Ecclesiastes expresses the voice of the soul in its three parts—emotion, will and mind. Psalms is the book of the heart. Proverbs is directed to the will, making its choices in life. Ecclesiastes is the penetrating inquiry of the mind, searching for answers.

What then is the Song of Solomon? It is preeminently the cry of the body in its essential yearning. That essential yearning is for love. From its birth our bodies cry out for love. They are made in such a way as to enjoy being touched, patted, caressed and embraced. Climaxing this capacity of the body for sensuous delight is the thrill of sexual intercourse. Therefore, the theme of this book is sexual intercourse between a man and his wife as the ultimate and purest expression of the divinely given function that we call sex. This book describes sex as God intended it to be, involving not merely physical exchange but touching the whole nature of two lives.

Freud was right about one thing—sex permeates our lives. He saw it as primarily physical and psychological, but it is even deeper. It is part of the expression of the human spirit as well. Someone has described the basic definition of sex as "the urge to merge." That urge finds its intended culmination with respect to the body in sexual play in marriage; with respect to the soul it finds delightful expression in friendship and social interchange; and with respect to God the "urge to merge" appears as worship, for the deepest desire of the heart is to be possessed by God and to possess Him. Surely this is what Jesus had in mind when He said in John 15 that the highest relationship He could have with His disciples would be "you in me and I in you" (see v. 4).

Because the Song of Solomon is about sexual love, it has been mistreated and often neglected. Victorian prudishness regarded sex as something dirty and not to be mentioned in polite company but kept locked in drawers and hidden behind curtains. That represents an extreme distortion of sexuality which has produced widespread hurtful responses in social life. The opposite view treats sex as something so commonplace it should be displayed without qualm and openly enjoyed whenever desired, with whatever partner is available. This too is extremely hurtful and produces social disaster.

But sex is not treated in either of these ways in the Bible; it is handled like every other subject, with frankness and forthrightness, yet with purity and restraint. Sexual love is never seen as pornographic or obscene in itself, but removed from the protection of marriage it becomes abused and ultimately emerges as something sordid and licentious. In the Song of Solomon we find the subject treated with delicate beauty and reflecting a wholesome delight in the joys of married sex.

The book comes to us as a musical play. The characters are Solomon, the young king of Israel, who at the beginning of his reign certainly must have manifested the finest qualities of the beauty and manliness of youth. In the complementary role is the Shulamite (the name is the feminine form of Solomon and we would translate it in modern language "Mrs. Solomon"). The play is set in Jerusalem, the capital of Israel, and is acted out before a chorus of singers referred to as "the daughters of Jerusalem." They ask certain leading questions from time to time, and on three occasions the Shulamite addresses them directly.

The book consists entirely of dialogue between the man and the woman with occasional side remarks directed to the chorus. This makes it difficult to piece together the background story, but certain verses give clues from time to time as to what the setting of the book is. At the end of the play in 8:11 we are told: "Solomon had a vineyard at Baal-hamon; he let out the vineyard to keepers; each one was to bring for its fruit a thousand pieces of silver." This suggests that the family of the young woman who is called the Shulamite evidently rented a tract of land from King Solomon located in the north country of Israel. The Shulamite is the Cinderella of the family. She has two brothers and two sisters but has been left to tend the flocks and to work in the vineyard herself. She spends her time out in the open sun all day, so that she becomes quite sunburned. In fact the book opens with her acknowledgement: "I am very dark, but comely, O daughters of Jerusalem, like the tents of Kedar, like the curtains of Solomon. Do not gaze at me because I am swarthy, because the sun has scorched me. My mother's sons were angry with me, they made me keeper of the vineyards; but, my own vineyard I have not kept!" (1:5-7).

As she works in the fields she watches the beautiful ladies of the court riding in their carriages up and down the road and envies them, but is quite content to remain in her humble life. One day she looks up to see a handsome stranger, a young shepherd lad looking at her very intently. She is disturbed by his gaze, but he says to her: "You are all fair, my love; there is no flaw in you" (4:7). That goes a long way in establishing a friendship, and they soon draw closer to each other.

As love dawns between them, they describe the beauty of each other in exquisite yet chaste language. Suddenly the young shepherd leaves, but before he goes he promises that he will return. Through the night she dreams of him and wishes for him, remembering his appearance and describing him to her friends.

Then one day there is a great commotion in the valley. The latter part of chapter 3 describes how excited the countryside is as King Solomon himself, with a company of sixty men of war, is seen coming up into the valley, riding in his royal carriage. To the amazement of everyone the king sends his riders to her house with the message that he desires to see her. She comes out shy and afraid and is brought to the royal pavilion. To her amazement she discovers that King Solomon is none other than her shepherd lover. He carries her away to his palace and they enter into a blissful state of communion and consummation together.

The language of the book is highly poetical and figurative and there may be some difficulty in determining who is the speaker, but it is helpful to remember (in the version we are following) that the bridegroom always refers to his bride as "my love" and she in return calls him "my beloved." Here is her description of him: "My beloved is all radiant and ruddy, distinguished among ten thousand. His head is the finest gold; his locks are wavy, black as a raven. His eyes are like doves beside springs of water, bathed in milk, fitly set. His cheeks are like beds of spices, yielding fragrance. His lips are lilies, distilling liquid myrrh. His arms are rounded gold, set with jewels. His body is ivory work, encrusted with sapphires. His legs are alabaster columns, set upon bases of gold. His appearance is like Lebanon, choice as the cedars. His speech is most sweet, and he is altogether desirable. This is my beloved and this is my friend, O daughters of Jerusalem" (5:10-16).

He describes her in similar language: "Behold, you are beautiful, my love, behold, you are beautiful! Your eyes are doves behind your veil. Your hair is like a flock of goats, moving down the slopes of Gilead. Your teeth are like a flock of shorn ewes that have come up from the washing, all of which bear twins, and not one among them is bereaved. Your lips are like a scarlet thread, and your mouth is lovely. Your cheeks are like halves of a pomegranate behind your veil. Your neck is like the tower of David, built for an arsenal, whereon hang a thousand bucklers, all of them shields of warriors. Your two breasts are like two fawns, twins of a gazelle, that feed among the lilies" (4:1-5).

It is important to see that the book describes married love as God intended it to be. The full abandonment to each other in mutual satisfaction which is described in this song is possible only because it is experienced within that total oneness which marriage alone permits. This is strongly emphasized throughout the book by the three-fold warning which the bride addresses to the unmarried girls in the chorus, referred to as "the daughters of Jerusalem." Three times, in 2:7, 3:5 and 8:4, the bride turns from her rapture and delight with her lover to give the secret of this delight: "I adjure you, O daughters of Jerusalem, by the gazelles or the hinds of the field, that you stir not up nor awaken love until it please." What does she mean? She means do not prematurely arouse love. Wait until it develops naturally in its own time. Do not stimulate it artificially before one is ready. Let love dawn of itself at its own unhurried pace. Surely much of the problem in today's broken marriages is a result of failing to heed this admonition. Fatuous mothers often encourage their small children to ape adults by teaching them to dance and even to date one another before they enter their teens. Without realizing what they are doing, they are awakening love before its time and it is no wonder that teenagers often enter into marriages for which they are almost totally unprepared. It is like trying to pry open a flower bud before it is ready to bloom. One simply destroys it.

The same is true of the practice of petting and necking. These too are ways of stimulating love before its time, and without doubt it has created serious problems of adjustment for young people entering into marriage. To young people, who truly desire the best out of love, this book teaches them to leave off such premarital stimulants and wait for the dawning of love in its own time. The Shulamite is able to say: "He brought me to the banqueting house, and his banner over me was love" (2:4). For her the consummation of love in marriage was like a banquet for which she had long been eagerly waiting and which fulfilled her anticipations to the very fullest degree.

Because the language of the book is strongly figurative, it is sometimes difficult for the Western mind to see the meaning of the figure employed. For instance, when the bridegroom says to the bride, "Your teeth are like a flock of shorn ewes that have come up from their washing, all of which bear twins, and not one among them is bereaved," he means that her beautiful teeth are full and complete and not one of them is missing. The actual act of sexual intercourse is referred to delicately by several euphemisms. One is that of coming into a garden. For instance: "Awake, O north wind, and come, O south wind! Blow upon my garden, let its fragrance be wafted abroad. Let my beloved come to his garden, and eat its choicest fruits. I come to my garden, my sister, my bride, I gather my myrrh with my spice, I eat my honeycomb with my honey, I drink my wine with my milk. Eat, O friends, and drink: drink deeply, O lovers!" (4:16—5:1).

Still another description of the act of love is climbing a palm tree; "How fair and pleasant you are, O loved one, delectable maiden! You are stately as a palm tree, and your breasts are like its clusters. I say I will climb the palm tree and lay hold of its branches. Oh, may your breasts be like clusters of the vine, and the scent of your breath like apples, and your kisses like the best wine that goes down smoothly, gliding over lips and teeth" (7:6-9).

God has ordained that the delights reflected here be a part of the experience of man and woman in marriage. To ignore this is to cheapen these delights and to make sex as commonplace as cutting one's fingernails. That which, with due restraint, is intended to be a rushing torrent of sensuous delight becomes instead a spreading flood in which one wades continually without pleasure.

This is clearly indicated toward the end of the book where reference is made to a sister of the bride: "We have a little sister, and she has no breasts. What shall we do for our sister, on the day when she is spoken for? If she is a wall, we will build upon her a battlement of silver; but if she is a door, we will enclose her with boards of cedar" (8:8,9). The little girl may be like a wall, that is, closed to easy friendships, resistant to the approaches of others. Her family then will respond by "building upon her a battlement of silver." A battlement is a sloping ramp by which a wall may be surmounted. In this case it was to be made of silver, which in Scripture is always a picture of redemption. The suggestion is that by teaching her the value of redemption by the love and grace of God she will be enabled to find a security that will safely accept the approaches of others and make her more open to communication.

However, "if she is a door, we will enclose her with boards of cedar." She may be like a door—open to all who come and far too easily influenced by others. In that case the role of the family is to protect her and enclose her with loving guidance that will enable her to grow and fully develop before she enters into marriage.

But of course we have not heard the deepest message of this song until we pass behind the description of purely physical love, perfect as it is, to read this as an expression of communion between man and God, between Christ and His church. From very earliest Christian centuries, this book has been taken in that way. Even the Jews took it allegorically in that sense. The preface to this song in one of the Jewish Targums reads like this: "This is the Song of Solomon, the prophet king of Israel, which he sang before Jehovah the Lord." This was not for them a purely human love song, but one to be sung before Jehovah. It was a song about one's own relationship with God. Certainly the early church fathers took it in that way, and throughout the Christian centuries this little book has been one of the most read and cherished books of all the Bible.

During the dark days before the Protestant Reformation, when the Albigenses fled the Catholic church and John Huss led his small band of Christians in Bohemia, this was one of the books of the Bible frequently read and quoted and memorized. It was a great comfort to the persecuted saints. After the Reformation, in the bitter persecution of the Covenanters of Scotland out of which came the Presbyterian church under the leadership of John Knox and others, this again was one of the most frequently quoted books. It brought the Covenanters great comfort and sustained the spirits of men and women who were hunted like animals throughout the mountains and glens of Europe.

Someone has well said, "If you love Jesus Christ, you will love this song, because here are words which fully express the rapture of the heart that has fallen in love with Christ." The message of the Song of Solomon is, metaphorically, that Christ is so wonderful, so magnificent, and the heart has so fallen in love with Him that it will never be possible to plumb the depths of Christ's love and concern and care. Every passage of this song can be reverently elevated to this higher level and seen as the expression of the heart enraptured with the Lord. Taken thus, it reveals a highly significant truth. As we read of the rapturous delight that the bride and the bridegroom experience in each other, we are also reading a magnificent and beautiful description of what God intends the relationship to be between Himself and each individual. Thus the great commandment is: "You shall love the Lord your God with all your heart, and with all your soul, and with all your mind (Matt. 22:37). Out of that love will flow every other love, including loving your neighbor as yourself.

In Paul's letter to the Ephesians he describes Christ as the true Bridegroom and His church as the bride, and says: "Husbands, love your wives, as Christ loved the church and gave himself up for her." And then he goes on to add: "This is a great mystery, and I take it to mean Christ and the church" (Eph. 5:25,32). So the love of a husband and wife pictures the love of Christ and His church. This in turn is a representation of the deep love God intends to exchange with each individual in a personal relationship together.

Listen, then, to these beautiful words of the bridegroom to the bride: "For lo, the winter is past, the rain is over and gone. The flowers appear on the earth, the time of singing has come, and the voice of the turtledove is heard in our land. The fig tree puts forth its figs, and the vines are in blossom; they give forth fragrance. Arise, my love, my fair one, and come away" (Song of Sol. 2:11-13).

There is described the springtime of life, but it does not lie in the past. It is in the future! One day this whole world will experience springtime. The Lord Jesus Christ returning at last to claim His waiting bride, will greet her with words very much like those. The springtime of earth will have come. The time of the singing has arrived. The time when the earth shall blossom and the curse will be lifted and flowers will appear on the land. But this is also a picture of what can take place in the heart of one who falls in love with Jesus Christ and thus enters into the spring-time of his life. The cold winter of loneliness, misery and selfishness is past and the time of the singing has come!

God Redeems

ISAIAH

The prophecy of Isaiah begins the last great division of the Old Testament—the 16 books of the prophets. We have already seen in the Old Testament that the first five books set out for us the *pattern of God's working in our lives*. These were followed by the historical books, Joshua through Esther. The major purpose of these is to detail the *perils which confront those seeking to walk with God* in the midst of a degenerate world. There we learned the power of the opposing forces of the spiritual life in their sly subtlety and cruel destructiveness, manifesting themselves in historical events. Then came the poetical books—Job through Song of Solomon—which express the *protests and rejoicings of the heart* exposed to the perils of the world. These books concentrate on the character of man and help us to understand ourselves in our threefold makeup of spirit, soul and body.

But now we come to the prophets. The pattern of life is given in the Pentateuch, the perils are set forth in the historical books, and the protests of the spirit and soul are expressed in the poetical books. But in the prophets we discover *the mighty promises of God*.

What is a promise? When two young people stand at a wedding altar while someone sings "O Promise Me," what are they doing? They are committing themselves to give of themselves to each other. A promise basically is a commitment to share yourself. In a promise you commit something of your time, your energy, your resources to another person. That is what a promise is; it is a sharing of self.

So the great promises of the Bible are God's commitments to share Himself with us. When we understand those promises we will understand something more of the nature and character of our God. That is why an understanding of the prophets is of such momentous importance in reading the Bible, for it is here we learn what God says He will do. It is impossible to exercise true faith if we do not have a promise upon which to rest our faith. People often prate on about faith and belief and yet never have any true basis or ground because they have no promise. If God has *said* He will do something, then we can exercise faith and expect Him to do it. If He has not said so, faith has no ground and is of no value.

Each of the prophetical books takes as its theme a great promise of God and highlights it in various ways, some like Isaiah in magnificent language, and others like Ezekiel in awesome imagery. Others employ powerful invectives or speak from weeping, grief-stricken hearts. But whatever the prophetic style, there gradually emerges through the prophetical books a vision of the character of God.

The prophets were all men who walked closely with God, and that is what enabled them to see into the heart of things, both present and future. As the priests of Israel sought to present men to God, so the prophets gave themselves to the ministry of presenting God to men.

In our English versions of the Old Testament, the first of the prophets is Isaiah. In many ways that order is representative of the man and his ministry, for Isaiah was the greatest of the prophets and a superb master of language.

This prophecy is the fullest revelation of Christ to be found in the Old Testament—so much so that it is frequently called "the gospel according to Isaiah." The book is often called a miniature Bible, for its structure parallels that of the whole Bible itself. As the Bible has 66 books, so Isaiah has 66 chapters. The Bible divides into two major divisions, the Old Testament and the New Testament, and Isaiah likewise divides into two major divisions. There are 39 books in the Old Testament and there are 39 chapters in the first section of Isaiah. There are 27 books in the New Testament and there are 27 chapters in the last half of Isaiah. Just as the New Testament begins with the history of John the Baptist the forerunner of Christ, so the second half of Isaiah at chapter 40 begins with the announcement of the coming of the forerunner. The New Testament ends with the book of Revelation with its vision of the new heaven and the new earth, while the book of Isaiah closes with a remarkable chapter that speaks also of the new heavens and the new earth God is now creating.

We know very little about Isaiah himself. He lived during the reigns of four kings of Judah—Uzziah, Jotham, Ahaz and Hezekiah. His ministry began some 740 years before Christ at a time when the 10 tribes that formed the northern kingdom of Israel were under attack from the Assyrian general, Sennacherib. At the close of Isaiah's ministry, Judah, the southern kingdom, was plunging into a terrible idolatry which would end with Nebuchadnezzar's attack and eventual captivity in Babylon. Thus the ministry of Isaiah spans the time between the captivity of the northern kingdom and the captivity of the southern kingdom—about 50 years duration. Ministering along with Isaiah during this same period of time were the prophets Amos, Hosea and Micah.

Tradition tells us that Isaiah was martyred in the reign of Manasseh, one of the most wicked of the kings recorded in the Old Testament. The story is that he was fleeing from the soldiers of the king and hid in a hollow tree, hoping to escape. But the soldiers, knowing that he was in the tree, sawed the tree down and thus the prophet was sawn in half. In the great chapter of the heroes of faith, Hebrews 11, verse 37, there is reference to some who perished by being sawn in two, and many scholars feel this refers to the prophet Isaiah.

The theme of the book is reflected in the meaning of the prophet's name: *Isaiah*—the salvation of God. It is the great and fundamental promise of all the Bible that God is able to redeem. It is declared most clearly in the opening chapter, verse 18: "Come now, let us reason together, says the Lord: though your sins are like scarlet, they shall be as white as snow; though they are red like crimson, they shall become like wool."

It is declared plainly again in chapter 55, verse 1: "Ho, every one who thirsts, come to the waters; and he who has no money, come, buy and eat! Come, buy wine and milk without money and without price."

Though these verses may be taken as a key to the book of Isaiah, nevertheless they must not lead us into thinking this book and other books of the Bible are like locked houses, barred and shuttered which cannot be entered unless a key is employed. Some people seem to feel that the only duly licensed real estate agents are Bible teachers and preachers who alone have keys to the Scriptures.

In 2 Peter, in the New Testament, Peter says: "But know this first of all, that no prophecy of Scripture is a matter of one's own interpretation, for no prophecy was ever made by an act of human will, but men moved by the Holy Spirit spoke from God" (1:20,21, *NASB*).

In this first letter, Peter had declared that "the prophets

who prophesied of the grace that would come to you made careful search and inquiry" (1:10, *NASB*). Thus we learn that prophets like Isaiah were very much aware that an invisible power within them was speaking through them and that what they spoke and wrote was greater than their own ideas. Peter goes on to say they actually searched through their own writings to discover hidden truths therein, and in this sense they ministered to themselves by their own prophecies.

The Search for Salvation

If any key is needed to the book of Isaiah, this is it: Isaiah was a man who was searching for something, and the apostle Peter tells us plainly that he was searching for the salvation which was to come from God.

But what set this man searching? Why does he pore over his writings, puzzling about what he had said? One need only open the book and read the first few chapters to find the answer. Isaiah lived in a time of national stress when man's fundamental nature of rebellion and evil was exposing itself for what it was. The nation had deliberately forsaken the ways of God and their stupid obstinacy is beyond the prophet's understanding. He opens the first chapter (v. 3) by saying: "The ox knows its owner, and the ass its master's crib; but Israel does not know, my people does not understand."

In various beautiful figures the prophet goes on to describe the condition of the nation in their self-deceptive reliance upon external religious activities while their hearts were given over to idolatry and sinful practices. There are gleams of promise in the midst of words of condemnation, such as the famous passage in chapter 2 (which also appears in the prophecy of Micah): "In the last days, the mountain of the house of the Lord will be established as the chief of the mountains, and will be raised above the hills; and all the nations will stream to it.

And many peoples will come and say, 'Come, let us go up to the mountain of the Lord, to the house of the God of Jacob; that He may teach us concerning His ways, and that we may walk in His paths" (2:2,3, *NASB*).

But before that beautiful promise is fulfilled, the terrible Day of the Lord must come, and Isaiah describes this both in its immediate fulfillment in the destruction of Jerusalem by Babylon and in its ultimate fulfillment in the last days of the age.

Chapter 5 contains the prophet's description of the nation as the vineyard of the Lord. It is to this passage that Jesus refers in the Upper Room Discourse in John 15 when He says: "I am the true vine and my Father is the vinedresser" (v. 1). Isaiah is puzzled how these two themes of condemnation and reconciliation can both be fulfilled, and he continues his search for an answer.

Then God gives Isaiah a vision and he sees the holy and pure God in an amazing revelation described in chapter 6: "In the year of King Uzziah's death, I saw the Lord sitting on a throne, lofty and exalted, with the train of His robe filling the temple. Seraphim stood above Him, each having six wings; with two he covered his face, and with two he covered his feet, and with two he flew. And one called out to another and said, 'Holy, Holy, Holy, is the Lord of hosts, the whole earth is full of His glory" (6:1-3, *NASB*).

In the year that King Uzziah died, when the throne was vacant, the prophet saw the throne that was never vacant. He saw the God of both wrath and power, the God with power to shake the earth to its foundations—an immense God, infinite and mighty, speaking in thunder and moving in strength. The prophet's reaction is to see his own sinfulness and cry out: "Woe is me! For I am lost; for I am a man of unclean lips, and I dwell in the midst of a people of unclean lips, for my eyes have seen the King, the Lord of hosts" (6:5).

But one of the angelic seraphim flies to him with a burning coal and touches his mouth and says: "Behold, this has touched your lips; your guilt is taken away, and your sin is forgiven" (v. 7). Thus in his own personal experience the prophet learns the secret of God's salvation: it is God Himself who must accomplish it, and man can have no part of it. Isaiah is then commissioned to go to the nation and cry to them, but is warned that they will not listen to his plea. When he asks how long this should go on the answer is: "Until cities are devastated and without inhabitant, houses are without people, and the land is utterly desolate (6:11, *NASB*).

God's Plan of Salvation

Beginning with chapter 7 through chapter 12 the first step in God's compassionate plan of salvation is revealed. When Ahaz, king of Judah, is troubled about threats to his kingdom from Syria and Samaria on the north, the prophet is sent to him with a message that God Himself will deliver the nation, and He will give them a sign: "Therefore the Lord Himself will give you a sign: Behold, a virgin will be with child and bear a son, and she will call His name Immanuel. He will eat curds and honey at the time He knows enough to refuse evil and choose good. For before the boy will know enough to refuse evil and choose good, the land whose two kings you dread will be forsaken" (7:14-16, *NASB*).

This, like many other prophecies in the Old Testament, finds a dual fulfillment. There is an immediate fulfillment described in chapter 8: "And I went to the prophetess, and she conceived and bore a son. Then the Lord said to me, 'Call his name Maher-shalal-hashbaz for before the child knows how to cry "My father" or "My mother," the wealth of Damascus and the spoil of Samaria will be carried away before the king of Assyria' " (8:3,4).

Here it is clear that God uses even the names of

Isaiah's two sons to convey his prophetic intent. An older son named *Sheari-jasheb* (a remnant shall return) had already signaled the promise that Judah would not be totally destroyed, but now *Maher-shalal-hashbaz* (swift the booty; speedy the prey) was to be a sign to King Ahaz that the two kings he feared would in themselves become booty and prey, fleeing swiftly before the Assyrian conquerors who would overcome them. And so it proved to be true.

The baby, who was the type of Immanuel, was not yet 12 years old before Damascus had been overthrown by a king of Assyria in 732, and Israel (Samaria) fell before the armies of Sargon II in 722 B.C. The Assyrian hordes so ravished the land of Palestine that the cultivated fields reverted to pasturage and the diet of Maher-shalal-hashbaz would therefore consist of curdled milk and honey rather than the more normal food.

But a further fulfillment centuries later is, without question, in view in this passage, for in chapter 9 the prophet's vision spans the centuries and settles upon a great blessing to come in the land of Galilee: "In earlier times He treated the land of Zebulun and the land of Naphthali with contempt, but later on He shall make it glorious, by the way of the sea, on the other side of Jordan, Galilee of the Gentiles. The people who walk in darkness will see a great light; those who live in a dark land, the light will shine on them" (9:1,2, *NASB*).

It is precisely this region which was to be the home of Jesus the Messiah, and it was from Galilee of the Gentiles that the light began to shine upon Israel in final fulfillment of the prophetic promise. Chapter 9 expands this promise by indicating that Messiah would be born as a human child. He would be of the line of David and yet would become the ultimate ruler of the earth. He would be God Himself and rule as Prince of Peace over the whole world, bestowing prosperity and peace upon the nations in the age to come. Thus the promise reaches even beyond the first coming of Jesus to the second coming as well, and to the millennial kingdom beyond.

The final vision of this section sees the judgment of God falling upon Assyria, who had been God's instrument to judge Samaria and Syria, but in turn became the deserved recipient of God's anger. Even here the judgment extends beyond the immediate fulfillment upon Syria in the eighth century B.C. and describes the ultimate judgment upon the man of sin who will appear in the last days, seen in foreview as the king of Assyria.

The section closes in chapter 11 with the prediction of a shoot coming from the stem of Jesse and a branch growing out of his roots, and of this promised One from the line of David the prophet sings: "And the Spirit of the Lord shall rest upon him, the spirit of wisdom and understanding, the spirit of counsel and might, the spirit of knowledge and the fear of the Lord. And his delight shall be in the fear of the Lord" (11:2,3).

These very words are fulfilled by Jesus in His ministry at Nazareth and all Galilee.

The Prediction of Judgments

A large section of the book, from chapters 13 through 23, is given over to judgments predicted upon the nations surrounding Judah. First the rising power of Babylon, which would ultimately overwhelm Assyria and become the greatest kingdom on earth; yet Babylon would ultimately fall to the Medes and the Persians and itself become an uninhabited ruin.

In chapter 14 the prediction of judgment again rises beyond the immediate earthly kingdom of Babylon and sees the satanic power which controls the earthly nations, describing the sin of Satan which occurred even before the foundation of the earth. "How you have fallen from heaven, O star of the morning, son of the dawn! You have been cut down to the earth, you who have weakened the nations! But you said in your heart, 'I will ascend to heaven; I will raise my throne above the stars of God, and I will sit on the mount of assembly in the recesses of the north. I will ascend above the heights of the clouds; I will make myself like the Most High' " (14:12-14, *NASB*).

Here the difference between the divine and human points of view is clearly evident. Man sees but the earthly kingdoms, the thrones which rise and fall through the passing centuries; but Scripture sees the satanic powers and angelic conflicts behind the earthly events. It is as Paul described in Ephesians 6: "For our struggle is not against flesh and blood, but against the rulers, against the powers, against the world forces of this darkness, against the spiritual forces of wickedness in the heavenly places" (v. 12, *NASB*).

Judgment is then pronounced upon Israel's ancient enemy, the Philistines, and upon their treacherous relative, Moab, on the eastern shores of the Dead Sea (chaps. 14 through 16). The power of Damascus and Ephraim (northern Israel) shall be brought to ruin, but a gleam of hope appears in the promise that Samaria would have a remnant of believers who would remain true to the living God.

Ethiopia and Egypt are then surveyed and both nations are warned of impending judgment from the Assyrian empire. However, in both cases an ultimate time of repentance and restoration through the mercies of God is predicted, and the final view of Egypt is that of a kingdom brought into godliness and true worship. These promises remain to be fulfilled at some future day (chaps. 18 and 19).

Again Babylon is described in its defeat by Medo-Persia and especially judgment upon her idols. Then Edom's destruction is foretold by the symbolic name, *Dumah*, which means "silent," representing the silence that will fall upon the land as its cities are left desolate and decayed. The Arabian tribes of Dedan and Kedar are put to flight by the conquering Assyrians, and ultimately even Jerusalem itself, in its careless gaiety, shall find its walls broken down and its citizens put under siege. The final burden of judgment falls upon Tyre, the commercial center of the world of the Mediterranean, because of her pride; and yet after 70 years she will be restored, as history confirms (chaps. 21-23).

Warning of Destruction

There follows in chapters 24-35 a series of sermons addressed to the leaders of the nation, giving warning upon warning of all-consuming destruction to come upon all classes of society if the present course of wickedness is not abandoned. Chapters 28 through 33 are especially severe, describing a series of "woes" which will come upon various classes within the nation for their continued unbelief and idolatry. The condition of the nation is described in vivid language: "These also reel with wine and stagger with strong drink; the priest and the prophet reel with strong drink, they are confused with wine, they stagger with strong drink; they err in vision, they stumble in giving judgment. For all tables are full of vomit, no place is without filthiness" (28:7,8).

An important passage here reveals God's method of teaching: "Whom will he teach knowledge, and to whom will he explain the message? Those who are weaned from the milk, those taken from the breast? For it is precept upon precept, precept upon precept, line upon line, line upon line, here a little, there a little" (vv. 9,10).

God does not give His message in orderly chapters as men do, with one chapter devoted to a single subject, but the Bible is written with a marvelous intermingling of truth, so that truth is always found balanced with other aspects of truth. This is why the expository study of

Scripture is so very important and helps to keep truth in the balance which is necessary to preserve from heresy.

Judah's condition is so bad, however, God must employ a special form of communication to reach those who are turning a deaf ear to His usual warning. Therefore the prophet goes on to say: "Indeed, He will speak to this people through stammering lips and a foreign tongue; He who said to them, 'Here is rest, give rest to the weary.' and, 'Here is repose,' but they would not listen" (vv. 11,12, *NASB*).

This is a reference to the coming Assyrian and Babylonian invasions of the land, filling the cities with strangers who will speak alien languages, as a grim confirmation that God keeps His word and punishes disobedience. This passage is quoted by the apostle Paul in chapter 14 of 1 Corinthians with reference to the gift of tongues, and shows that the purpose of that gift is one of judgment upon the people who should have been the conveyors of the message of deliverance to the nation but who instead were living only for selfish interests. As the apostle states, such strange tongues are "a sign to unbelievers" (see v. 22). The tongues on the Day of Pentecost were such a sign, indicating that God was turning away from a favored position with Israel to the Gentile nations of the world.

But amidst the warnings to Judah there is a radiant burst of promise to those who remain faithful, for the prophet declares that God will lay in Zion a foundation stone, a precious cornerstone who will be utterly trustworthy and who will provide a basis for salvation to individuals and to the nation. Clearly this reference looks ahead to the coming of the Messiah, for Jesus Himself declared that He was that cornerstone.

Further vivid warnings are given, especially to those who seek to rely upon the help of Egypt or any other human aid other than the divine promise. The terrible Day of the Lord is described in frightening terms as crushing both human enemies and the satanic powers which are behind them. But the section closes with a beautiful passage in which God's promise of restoration is described: "Strengthen the weak hands, and make firm the feeble knees. Say to those who are of a fearful heart, 'Be strong, fear not! Behold, your God will come with vengeance, with the recompense of God. He will come and save you.' Then the eyes of the blind shall be opened, and the ears of the deaf unstopped; then shall the lame man leap like a hart, and the tongue of the dumb sing for joy. For waters shall break forth in the wilderness, and streams in the desert" (35:3-6).

An Historical Interlude

An historic interlude appears in chapters 36-39 which is recorded in prose style rather than in the poetic form of the rest of the book. It centers upon King Hezekiah, the last of the four kings during whose reign Isaiah prophesied. Rabshakeh, the arrogant general of the king of Assyria, has led a great army against Israel and Judah. Having laid waste the cities of Judah, he now stands before the walls of Jerusalem and impudently demands the surrender of the city. When the report of this demand was brought to King Hezekiah he tore his clothes and covered himself with sackcloth and went into the Temple of the Lord. From there he sent word to the prophet Isaiah and the prophet returned a reassuring word that the king was not to be afraid, for God would cause the general to return to Assyria, and this was shortly fulfilled.

However, the king of Assyria renewed the assault and sent an arrogant letter to King Hezekiah again demanding the surrender of the city under pain of its total destruction. Hezekiah took the letter into the Temple and spread it before the Lord and prayed humbly for God's intervention. Again the prophetic word was given that God Himself would defend the city and would keep it safe from the

Assyrian assault. That very night the angel of the Lord
came among the Assyrians and slew 185,000 in one night.
History records it as a great plague which suddenly broke
out in the camp. After this, Sennacherib, the king of
Assyria, departed to his own land where he was murdered
by two of his sons and another son, Esar-haddon, reigned
in his stead.

Following this great deliverance, King Hezekiah fell
sick and Isaiah was sent to him with the word that he was
to set his house in order for he would surely die. But once
again Hezekiah turned in prayer to the Lord and besought
Him for restoration. Once again the prophet Isaiah was
sent to the king but this time with a message of mercy and
a promise of recovery. Fifteen years additional life had
been granted to the king because of his repentance, and as
a sign of this divine mercy a remarkable event took place.
The shadow on the sun dial in the king's garden turned
backward 10 degrees. This meant that the day was lengthened by several hours and would have required a shift in
the direction of the axis of the earth. The biblical account
does not record any of the results of this in nature, but
scientists have learned that there have been times in the
past when the earth changed its axial direction, with
remarkable suddenness. This event was surely intended to
impress King Hezekiah that the God whom he served was
the God of life and of death, of time and eternity, and in
control of all events and circumstances of earth.

But the significance of it seemed to be lost upon the
king, for chapter 39 begins the account of how the king of
Babylon sent envoys with letters and presents to Hezekiah
after he had recovered from his illness and the foolish king
took the Babylonian ambassadors into the treasure house
of the palace and showed him all his wealth. When Isaiah
heard of this he said to the king: "Hear the word of the
Lord of hosts: Behold, the days are coming, when all that
is in your house, and that which your fathers have stored

up till this day, shall be carried to Babylon; nothing shall be left, says the Lord" (39:5,6).

Thus the first half of the prophecy of Isaiah ends with a shadow of ultimate captivity darkening the future, despite the partial recovery of the nation under Hezekiah.

Salvation Revealed

The last 27 chapters of the book (40-66) present in magnificent language the answer to Isaiah's long search for the salvation of Jehovah. Woven beautifully throughout the book has been the ever-growing revelation of God's love and promise of salvation to be realized in the figure of One who is to come—the Messiah, the Servant of Jehovah. At first that figure is dim and shadowy, but gradually it grows brighter and still brighter until in chapter 53 the Suffering Servant who accomplishes the ultimate salvation of God's people fills the whole horizon. It was given to Isaiah to show that the God of transcendent glory, whom he described in chapter 6, is the same God who would one day be "despised and rejected by men; a man of sorrows, and acquainted with grief; and as one from whom men hide their faces" (53:3).

Isaiah saw how God's love would break the back of man's rebelliousness and, despite his stubborn perversity, would open a way of recovery and restoration.

Then at last, beyond the darkness and gloom of the centuries yet to come, there would be a morning without clouds, the Day of Righteousness when all of God's glory would fill the earth and man would make war no more. They would beat their swords into pruning hooks and their spears into plows, and nothing would hurt or destroy in all God's holy mountain. This is the magnificent theme of chapters 40-66.

It begins in chapter 40 with a word of comfort declared to the suffering nation and the promise of the appearance of one who would be the forerunner, who would cry in the wilderness: "Prepare the way of the Lord, make straight in the desert a highway for our God" (40:3). These words were clearly fulfilled by John the Baptist as recorded in the Gospels. The prophet extolls the majesty and the greatness of God and contrasts Him with the puny insignificance of the idols whom the people have given themselves to worship. Then in chapter 42 the Servant of Jehovah is clearly introduced: "Behold my servant, whom I uphold, my chosen, in whom my soul delights; I have put my Spirit upon him, he will bring forth justice to the nations. He will not cry or lift up his voice, or make it heard in the street; a bruised reed he will not break, and a dimly burning wick he will not quench; he will faithfully bring forth justice. He will not fail or be discouraged till he has established justice in the earth; and the coastlands wait for his law" (42:1-4).

In chapters 43-48 the prophet describes in majestic and marvelous language the unchanging love of God for His people and the power and providential wisdom of God in working out His strange ways through the nations of earth to accomplish His ultimate purposes of redemption and grace.

But in chapters 49-57 the Servant of Jehovah occupies the whole horizon of prophetic vision. First He appears in His birth and early life: "Listen to me, O coastlands, and hearken, you peoples from afar. The Lord called me from the womb, from the body of my mother he named my name. He made my mouth like a sharp sword, in the shadow of his hand he hid me; he made me a polished arrow, in his quiver he hid me away. And he said to me, 'You are my servant, Israel, in whom I will be glorified' " (49:1-3).

Then His character and ministry are described: "The Lord God has given me the tongue of those who are taught, that I may know how to sustain with a word him that is weary. Morning by morning he wakens, he wakens my ear to hear as those who are taught. The Lord God has opened my ear, and I was not rebellious, I turned not backward. I gave my back to the smiters, and my cheeks to those who pulled out the beard; I hid not my face from shame and spitting" (50:4-6).

This prophetic anticipation of the close communion between Jesus and His heavenly Father is expanded in succeeding chapters and is met by the joyful response of those who are touched by the messianic hand of deliverance: "How beautiful upon the mountains are the feet of him who brings good tidings, who publishes peace, who brings good tidings of good, who publishes salvation, who says to Zion, 'Your God reigns' " (52:7).

Then in full and glorious vision the description of the actual atoning sacrifice is presented: "But he was wounded for our transgressions, he was bruised for our iniquities; upon him was the chastisement that made us whole, and with his stripes we are healed. All we like sheep have gone astray; we have turned every one to his own way; and the Lord has laid on him the iniquity of us all. He was oppressed, and he was afflicted, yet he opened not his mouth; like a lamb that is led to the slaughter, and like a sheep that before its shearers is dumb, so he opened not his mouth" (53:5-7).

The passage goes on to imply clearly a resurrection after the suffering and death, for the prophet states: "When he makes himself an offering for sin, he shall see his offspring, he shall prolong his days; the will of the Lord shall prosper in his hand; he shall see the fruit of the travail of his soul and be satisfied" (53:10,11).Nowhere in all the Bible is there a more lucid view of the person and work of the Redeemer than here in the fifty-third chapter of Isaiah! Here, as Peter says, the prophet saw clearly "the sufferings of Christ" (see 1 Pet. 1:11).

But in equally clear vision Isaiah sees beyond to "the glory which should follow." Chapter 54 opens with the triumphant exhortation to those who have entered into the redemption provided so freely but at such great cost. "Sing, O barren one, who did not bear; break forth into singing and cry aloud, you who have not been in travail! For the children of the desolate one will be more than the children of her that is married, says the Lord" (54:1).

The glorious invitation to all who would partake is extended in chapter 55: "Ho, every one who thirsts, come to the waters; and he who has no money, come, buy and eat! Come, buy wine and milk without money and without price. Why do you spend your money for that which is not bread, and your labor for that which does not satisfy? Hearken diligently to me, and eat what is good, and delight yourselves in fatness" (55:1,2).

The final chapters from 56-66 are given over primarily to the description of the glory and peace that shall come to the earth when God's King reigns in righteousness. This is also of course fulfilled in the individual within the redeemed spirit. It thus has both a symbolic and a literal fulfillment. Listen to the magnificent language of this promise: "For you shall go out in joy, and be led forth in peace; the mountains and the hills before you shall break forth into singing, and all the trees of the field shall clap their hands. Instead of the thorn shall come up the cypress; instead of the brier shall come up the myrtle; and it shall be to the Lord for a memorial, for an everlasting sign which shall not be cut off" (55:12,13).

The promise of restoration to the nation Israel, the fulfillment of all God declared to David, is clearly stated in chapter 60: "Foreigners shall build up your walls, and their kings shall minister to you; for in my wrath I smote you, but in my favor I have had mercy on you. Your gates shall be open continually; day and night they shall not be shut; that men may bring to you the wealth of the nations, with their kings led in procession. For the nation and kingdom that will not serve you shall perish; those nations shall be utterly laid waste" (60:10-12).

Again in the same chapter the beautiful description continues: "The sun shall be no more your light by day, nor for brightness shall the moon give light to you by night; but the Lord will be your everlasting light, and your God will be your glory. Your sun shall no more go down, nor your moon withdraw itself; for the Lord will be your everlasting light, and your days of mourning shall be ended. Your people shall all be righteous; they shall possess the land for ever" (60:19-21).

As in the book of Revelation, where John the Seer cries out in the closing words, "Even so, come, Lord Jesus!" so Isaiah ends his prophecy with the prayer of God's people crying: "O that thou wouldst rend the heavens and come down, that the mountains might quake at thy presence—as when fire kindles brushwood and the fire causes water to boil—to make thy name known to thy adversaries, and that the nations might tremble at thy presence!" (64:1,2).

Finally, the ultimate end is achieved: "For behold, I create new heavens and a new earth; and the former things shall not be remembered or come into mind. But be glad and rejoice for ever in that which I create" (65:17,18).

Before this beautiful day arrives a time of final judgment must be consummated, and the prophet describes it: "For behold, the Lord will come in fire, and his chariots like the stormwind, to render his anger in fury, and his rebuke with flames of fire. For by fire will the Lord execute judgment, and by his sword, upon all flesh; and those slain by the Lord shall be many" (66:15,16).

But the final scene is one of eternal peace: "For as the new heavens and the new earth which I will make shall remain before me, says the Lord; so shall your descendants and your name remain. From new moon to new moon, and from sabbath to sabbath, all flesh shall come to worship before me, says the Lord" (66:22,23).

Thus the great prophecy of Isaiah presents the theme of all the prophets, the majesty of God and the greatness of His redemptive love. But more clearly than anywhere else in the Old Testament the prophet Isaiah is given to see the divine-human Servant of the Lord who presents His body as an atonement for the sins of God's people and through His suffering obtains a salvation which, entered into by faith, brings deliverance and ultimate restoration of beauty and grace to the individual and to all the earth.

CHAPTER SIX

God Chastens

JEREMIAH

What would be the reaction of the congregation if some present-day American stood in his pulpit and persistently declared God was on the side of the Communist bloc nations and against America? Suppose he claimed divine inspiration in declaring that God was raising up the Russians to be His servants for the destruction of the United States. And further, that God cared nothing for the Declaration of Independence or the American Constitution or the heritage of religious worship which our nation has experienced. In fact, emphasis on these things were an offense to God.

And what if this preacher even advocated that Christians renounce their loyalty to their country and join the Communist bloc of nations? What if that preacher were to be subjected to house arrest, flung into prison, even slapped in the face in public and his writings burned, and he himself half-drowned in a pit of slime—yet he would not take back one word of what he had said, but stubbornly repeated it again? If this should occur it would have a very similar impact to that recorded in the prophecy of Jeremiah! This was the experience of Jeremiah the prophet.

Imagine yourself as that preacher. Imagine how you would feel when you preached your heart out but no one would listen, and persecution hounded you every way you turned. You are unable to seek comfort in marriage because the days are too difficult and God has specifically told you to remain unmarried. You feel abandoned and alone. All your friends turn from you. But if you try to quit, and refuse to preach, you find that you cannot quit—that the word of God burns in your bones and you have to speak it whether or not you want to. Despite the message of judgment you are called upon to deliver, your love for your country is genuine and deep. As you see it surrounded by its enemies, ravished, conquered and despoiled, you are overcome by a deep sorrow that breaks out in the lamentations of grief.

If you can imagine such a situation, you will understand why Jeremiah, of all the prophets, was unquestionably the most heroic. Isaiah spoke in more exalted language and saw more in detail the coming of the Messiah and the fullness of His work. Others of the prophets speak more specifically concerning future events to be fulfilled. But Jeremiah is outstanding among the prophets as a man of heroic and dauntless courage. For almost 50 years he endured the kind of persecution we have described, and yet he never gave up!

Jeremiah lived in the last days of the southern kingdom of Judah. Isaiah had finished his ministry about 60 years before Jeremiah came on the scene. Jeremiah ministered at the close of the reign of the last good king of Judah, the boy king Josiah who led the last revival the nation experienced before it went into captivity. His ministry carried on through the reign of King Jehoahaz and through King Jehoiakim—one of the most evil kings Judah had. Jehoiakim was followed by the three-month reign of Jehoiachin (also called Coniah), who was taken by Nebuchadnezzar and brought into captivity in Babylon. Jeremiah's ministry continued through the reign of Judah's last king, Zedekiah, who reigned until Nebuchadnezzar returned and utterly destroyed Jerusalem, taking the entire nation into Babylonian captivity.

Unfortunately, the messages of the prophet which appear in this book are not arranged in chronological sequence, especially in the latter part of the book. The Greek version (the Septuagint) shows considerable difference from the Hebrew text of Jeremiah. We learn from the book itself that Jeremiah dictated his prophecy to his secretary Baruch (see 36:4-8), and the disorderly arrangement of the messages may possibly be accounted for by the confusion attendant upon Jeremiah's flight to Egypt.

Two important emphases are woven into the fabric of this entire book. One concerns the *fate of the nation*. The other concerns the *feelings of the prophet*. Both are exceedingly instructive to us. The first chapter of the prophecy recounts the call and commissioning of Jeremiah to his prophetic office. He was only a young man, probably in his late teens or perhaps 20 years of age when he was set aside for his prophetic task. Like Moses at the burning bush, Jeremiah protested his commission and pleaded that he was too young for the immense task set before him, but God gave him clear answer: "Behold, I have put my words in your mouth. See, I have set you this day over nations and over kingdoms, to pluck up and to break down, to destroy and to overthrow, to build and to plant" (1:9,10).

In the first of many parabolic figures which appear in the book as helpful visual aids, the young prophet is shown the vision of an almond tree which is the first of the fruitbearing trees to bloom in the early spring. Because the Hebrew word for *almond* is very close to the word for *watcher*, the prophet is told that the almond branch is a symbol of God's watchfulness over His word to perform all that He said in precise detail. Jeremiah is then shown a vision of a boiling pot, facing away from the north, and this is interpreted to be a picture of the tumultuous trouble that will come upon the land of Judah from a northern kingdom. These introduce the themes of the entire prophecy. The prophet himself is encouraged to speak regardless of what the reaction of his hearers may be, for God says: "And I, behold, I make you this day a fortified city, an iron pillar, and bronze walls, against the whole land, against the kings of Judah, its princes, its priests, and the people of the land. They will fight against you; but they shall not prevail against you, for I am with you, says the Lord, to deliver you" (1:18,19).

Condemnation of Judah's Apostasy

As with many of the prophets, Jeremiah's early messages, recorded in the first 13 chapters, consist largely of condemnation of Judah's apostasy and earnest pleas for repentance while there is yet time before judgment falls. The major figure employed is that of a bride with her husband whom she forsakes and turns to many strange lovers. For this reason God calls Judah a prostitute, for the Baal worship which she was indulging in involved many foul sexual practices.

In a similar manner Israel, the northern kingdom, had fallen into idolatry and had been sent into exile which the prophets likened to being "divorced" by the Lord. But in spite of this vivid example, Judah persists in her idolatrous behavior, and though she attempts to win God's favor by an outward show of religion, it is but a sham repentance and neither God nor His prophet Jeremiah is deceived by it. The lion from Babylon is stalking its prey and soon Jerusalem will be laid under siege. It is not a cruel and heartless God who brings that about, but Jeremiah plainly declares to the people of Judah: "Your ways and your doings have brought this upon you. This is your doom, and it is bitter; it has reached your very heart" (4:18).

Nor does the prophet deliver these messages with unfeeling indifference. When his prophetic vision sees the coming judgment he cries out: "My anguish, my anguish! I writhe in pain! Oh, the walls of my heart! My heart is beating wildly; I cannot keep silent; for I hear the sound of the trumpet, the alarm of war" (4:19). In beautiful poetic discourse the prophet describes in detail the sight of the invading armies of the north and the terror they create as they enter the land, though it will be several decades before this fierce judgment ultimately falls, for God is a very patient God and waits until the last possible moment for genuine repentance from His people. Nevertheless, the prophet knows that judgment is inevitable, for he sees the events of his day from the divine viewpoint.

He is told by the Lord concerning his own ministry: "I have made you an assayer and tester among my people, that you may know and assay their ways" (6:27). But such clear vision only means deeper anguish on the prophet's part, for he sees how blind the people are to their own peril and how they turn a deaf ear to all words of warning.

An example of this is found in chapters 7-10. The prophet is sent by the Lord to stand in a gate of the Temple and proclaim a great message of warning to the people who trust in their ritual—and in the fact that the Temple was God's earthly home—to protect them from any judgment. To them the prophet said: "Behold, you trust in deceptive words to no avail. Will you steal, murder, commit adultery, swear falsely, burn incense to Baal, and go after other gods that you have not known, and then come and stand before me in this house, which is called by my name, and say, 'We are delivered!'—only to go on doing all these abominations? Has this house, which is called by my name, become a den of robbers in your eyes? Behold, I myself have seen it, says the Lord" (7:8-11).

In vivid and forthright words the prophet describes their foul idolatrous practices and warns them that exile is certain unless they change. The prophet identifies himself deeply with the people's fate, crying: "O that my head were waters, and my eyes a fountain of tears, that I might weep day and night for the slain of the daughter of my people!" (9:1).

In the midst of this great Temple message there are many wise words of counsel, such as: "Thus says the Lord: 'Let not the wise man glory in his wisdom, let not the mighty man glory in his might, let not the rich man glory in his riches; but let him who glories glory in this, that he understands and knows me, that I am the Lord who practice steadfast love, justice, and righteousness in the earth; for in these things I delight, says the Lord' " (9:23,24). Also, with keen awareness of the nature of fallen humanity, the prophet says: "I know, O Lord, that the way of man is not in himself, that it is not in man who walks to direct his steps" (10:23).

Chapters 11-13 highlight the fact that God's judgment of His faithless people rests upon the broken covenant which Israel as a nation had accepted at Sinai. There Moses had faithfully warned them of the consequences of turning from their relationship with God; and now in Judah those terrible results were hovering on the horizon of national life. They were so far advanced in their stubborn rebellion that the prophet is told not to pray for them any longer, for judgment was now inevitable.

Prayer has the effect of delaying judgment, but delay is not helpful unless it can lead to repentance. In this case long delay had not awakened a true repentance in the people and God knows that only a severe hand of punishment can awaken them to their true condition. It is evident that nations, like individuals, can sin "the sin which is unto death" (see 1 John 5:16). Physical judgment cannot be averted even by prayer, because it is the only way to at last reach the stubborn and wilfully rebellious heart.

The prophet employs in this section two vividly enacted parables to impress upon the people the impact of his message. He is sent by the Lord to buy a pair of linen undershorts and to go to the Euphrates River and hide them in the dirt. Then after several weeks he was to recover the rotted cloth and display it before the people, with the words: "Thus says the Lord: Even so will I spoil the pride of Judah and the great pride of Jerusalem. This evil people, who refuse to hear my words, who stubbornly follow their own heart and have gone after other gods to serve them and worship them, shall be like this waist-cloth, which is good for nothing. For as the waistcloth clings to the loins of a man, so I made the whole house of Israel and the whole house of Judah cling to me, says the Lord, that they might be for me a people, a name, a praise, and a glory, but they would not listen" (13:9-11).

Full wine jars are also employed as a parable of the stupefaction and bewilderment which possessed the people who, like drunken men, fall helpless to the ground, unable to rise.

God Prohibits Jeremiah's Intercession

Further symbols are used as vivid visual aids by the prophet in the section from chapters 14 through 19. Once again the prophet is told not to intercede for the people, for the Lord will not hear their cry even though they offer burnt offerings and sacrifices, for He knows their hearts. In fact God says that even though Moses and Samuel stood before Him, yet their intercession would not effect deliverance for this stubborn people.

This seemingly heartless stance finds immediate effect upon the prophet, who cries out in protest: "Thy words were found, and I ate them, and thy words became to me a joy and the delight of my heart; for I am called by thy name, O Lord, God of hosts" (15:16).

But despite his joy in the word of the Lord, he cannot reconcile this with the refusal of God to allow intercession for the people, and so he cries again: "Why is my pain unceasing, my wound incurable, refusing to be healed? Wilt thou be to me like a deceitful brook, like waters that fail?" (15:18).

But Jehovah is merciful with His overwrought prophet, and says: "If you return, I will restore you, and you shall stand before me. If you utter what is precious, and not what is worthless, you shall be as my mouth. They shall turn to you, but you shall not turn to them. And I will make you to this people a fortified wall of bronze; they will fight against you, but they shall not prevail over you, for I am with you to save you and deliver you, says the Lord. I will deliver you out of the hand of the wicked, and redeem you from the grasp of the ruthless" (15:19-21).

Because of the troubles which were coming upon the land and the resentment which Jeremiah's message would arouse, the Lord commanded him to remain unmarried, though it would mean loneliness and pain to the prophet. He is given great insight into the troubled character of fallen humanity and is encouraged to deal resolutely and realistically with life as it truly is, for he is told: "The heart is deceitful above all things, and desperately corrupt; who can understand it? I the Lord search the mind and try the heart, to give to every man according to his ways, according to the fruit of his doings" (17:9,10).

But to encourage him, in chapter 18 the prophet is sent to visit the house of the potter and there to observe the potter at work. He watches him take a lump of clay and shape from it a vessel. As the prophet watches, the vessel in the potter's hand is marred and broken. Then the potter takes the broken vessel and forms it again into a lump of clay to reshape it into a vessel, true and perfect according to the potter's design.

So the prophet was taught by this object lesson what

God does with a broken life, whether it be a nation or an individual. He can take it and make it over, not according to the foolish dreams of an individual, but according to His own heart, for the potter has power over the clay to shape it as he wishes. So Jeremiah spoke a prophecy of ruin, desolation, destruction and judgment; nevertheless beyond the judgment would lie the hope of the glory of God when God would reshape the vessel and make it according to His desire.

Jeremiah's faithful preaching in the public courts of the Temple was not taken lightly. Chapter 20 records how Pashhur the priest, chief officer of the Temple, seized the prophet and beat him and put him in stocks, but when he is released the next morning Jeremiah proceeds again to prophesy. The courage of this prophet is amazing, for when he is in the public eye he is fearless as a lion. He speaks to kings and captains and even hired murderers who hurl enraged threats against him, and he is utterly fearless! He looks them right in the eye and delivers the message of God, even when it predicts their own destruction. But when he is alone with God, he is filled with discouragement and depression and bitterness, and it all comes flooding out.

After his encounter with Pashhur, the prophet pours out his troubled heart to the Lord. He determines not to preach any more, but says: "If I say, 'I will not mention him, or speak any more in his name,' there is in my heart as it were a burning fire shut up in my bones, and I am weary with holding it in, and I cannot" (20:9). Like Job, he curses the day he was born, and wishes that the Lord would take pity upon him and end his days on earth. The problem is, of course, that he has forgotten what God has promised to be to him; but when he remembers his God, his despair passes and he realizes that his adversaries cannot ultimately prevail against him.

Prophecies of Exile and Restoration

In the section, chapters 21-39, there is a collection of messages from the prophet uttered during the reign of King Jehoiakim and the last king of Judah, Zedekiah. They are not found in chronological order, but contain many items of interest within them.

Before King Zedekiah, as recorded in chapter 21, the prophet foretells the victory of the Babylonian forces who are besieging the city, and announces that the king himself will be taken captive. He urges the people to go out of the city and surrender to the Chaldeans. This message was of course regarded as treason by the leaders of the nation, and plots were laid to trap Jeremiah and put him to death.

The short three-months reign of Jehoiachin, the son of Jehoiakim, is covered. This king is also called Coniah, and in chapter 22 an important thing is said about him by the prophet: "Thus says the Lord: 'Write this man down as childless, a man who shall not succeed in his days; for none of his offspring shall succeed in sitting on the throne of David, and ruling again in Judah' " (22:30). The fulfillment of this prediction meant an end to the dynasty of the descendants of King Solomon. His uncle, Zedekiah, was the last king of that line to sit upon the throne, and since that time no king of the Solomonic line has occupied the throne in Israel.

In the New Testament, Joseph, the stepfather of Jesus, comes from the line of kings which trace back through Jehoiachin, but that line has lost its right to reign. It is for this reason that the genealogy of Mary is traced by Luke and indicates descent from David through another of his sons, not Solomon. It is through David's son Nathan that the royal line is continued, and Mary thus passes on to her son Jesus the right to the throne, thus evading the curse placed upon Jehoiachin.

In chapter 23, Jeremiah sees across the centuries and describes the outworking of God's ultimate plan for His people: "Behold, the days are coming, says the Lord, when I will raise up for David a righteous Branch, and he shall reign as king and deal wisely, and shall execute justice and righteousness in the land. In his days Judah will be saved, and Israel will dwell securely. And this is the name by which he will be called: 'The Lord is our righteousness' " (23:5,6).

Chapter 24 employs another vivid visual aid in the figure of two baskets of figs which have been brought to the Temple as first-fruits. One basket is filled with good figs and the other with rotten. The good figs represent the exiled from Judah which are taken to Babylon but who are godly in heart and continue to worship the Lord there. Promises are given of encouragement to them. The bad figs represent Zedekiah and the leaders of the nation who remain in the land and become a curse to the nation, bringing warfare, famine and pestilence upon the land.

In chapter 25 the great prophecy of the 70 years of captivity is found. Most scholars compute this as beginning in 605 B.C. when the first deportation to Babylon took place. This would bring the end of the 70 years in 538 B.C. with the decree of Cyrus the Persian for the return of the remnant to the land, recorded in the book of Ezra. It was this very prophecy of Jeremiah which young Daniel, one of the royal captives in the land of Babylon, studied and understood from it when the 70 years would end. As the time drew near, he based his prayer for restoration upon the promise of God to end their captivity within 70 years.

Chapter 26 is a flashback to the days of King Jehoiakim at the beginning of the ministry of Jeremiah, and records his contest with certain false prophets in the royal court.

Chapters 27 and 28 leap ahead to Zedekiah, the last king of Judah, and describe the prophet's conflict with the false prophets in Zedekiah's reign, especially Hananiah, who had prophesied to the king that Babylon would soon be defeated and the Temple vessels returned to Jerusalem. He claimed divine inspiration for his prophecy, and in answering, Jeremiah predicts the death of Hananiah as a sign of his false ministry. Within the year the prophet died, but the people seemed to be unimpressed by this dramatic sign.

By this time a considerable number of exiles had already been carried to Babylon, and the prophet sought to encourage them by writing them a letter, recorded in chapter 29. Certain false prophets among the Jews in Babylon were predicting a speedy return to Jerusalem, but Jeremiah warned them that their captivity must last out the entire 70-year period predicted. During this time they were to marry and raise families, build houses and work for the welfare of the land in which they found themselves captive.

Chapters 30-33 are the heart of the prophecy, and in this section Jeremiah seems to see with clear vision the days of restoration after the judgment of Israel. In the peculiar way of prophets, he extends his view from immediate events to those far distant, even beyond the ultimate dispersion of the people of Israel to the final regathering of the nation into the land.

In this section is found the promise of the new covenant, to be applied to the united nations of Israel and Judah. This new covenant is what is called in Hebrews 13:20 "the eternal covenant," and is what the Lord Jesus referred to when, at the Last Supper, He took the cup and said, "This is my blood of the [new] covenant, which is poured out for many for the forgiveness of sins" (Matt. 26:28) The new covenant is the promise of an indwelling power and a full forgiveness which enables individuals to fulfill the law and walk in unbroken fellowship with a holy God. Hebrews 8 makes clear that it is the privilege of believers today to live in the power of the new covenant by faith, but one day that blessed promise will be worked out for the entire nation of Israel, as the apostle Paul confirms in Romans 11.

This new covenant is so sure in its fulfillment as applied to the nation that Jeremiah is told that while the sun gives light by day and the moon and the stars by night he may rest assured that God will fulfill His word and carry out His promises to His people.

This beautiful vision of restoration was given to Jeremiah during a time of great personal pressure. The Babylonian army was besieging Jerusalem and Jeremiah had been shut up in the court of the palace of King Zedekiah because he had predicted that the city would fall to the Babylonians, but while Jeremiah was a prisoner God sent his cousin to him to arrange for Jeremiah to purchase a field in his hometown of Anathoth and to record the deed very carefully in the legal records of the kingdom. This was a seemingly foolish action in light of the present circumstances, for what good are legal deeds when an army is pounding at the doors ready to carry the people off into captivity? But Jeremiah rightly saw it as a promise of God that the nation would be restored and that when the days of captivity were ended the deeds would again be valid.

Once again the prophet is given a vision of the coming Messiah and the days of fulfillment which await the nation: "Behold, the days are coming, says the Lord, when I will fulfil the promise I made to the house of Israel and the house of Judah. In those days and at that time I will cause a righteous Branch to spring forth for David; and he shall execute justice and righteousness in the land. In those days Judah will be saved and Jerusalem will dwell securely. And this is the name by which it will be called: 'The LORD is our righteousness' " (33:14-16).

Chapters 34-39 again are not in consecutive order but concern certain relationships which the prophet had with two of the kings of Judah, Zedekiah and Jehoiakim. Chapter 34 especially gives a keen perspective on what God expects of kings in relationship with their subjects, and emphasizes the divine view of human slavery. King Zedekiah took back the slaves which he had freed in accordance with the word of the Lord in Deuteronomy, and he is accused by the prophet of having thus "profaned the name of the Lord" (see v. 16). Thus mistreatment of other human beings is clearly regarded as an insult to the divine name and will. For this the king was to suffer greatly in Babylon.

Chapters 35 and 36 concern an earlier incident during the reign of Jehoiakim. One concerns the family of the Rechabites, who seem to be the forerunners of modern gypsies. Another important incident describes how King Jehoiakim deliberately destroyed the scroll of prophetic revelation which came to him from Jeremiah by the hand of Baruch, Jeremiah's servant. Insolently the king took his pen knife and cut the scroll in pieces, throwing them into the fire, thus indicating his contempt for the word of God. We are told: "Then Jeremiah took another scroll and gave it to Baruch the scribe, the son of Neriah, who wrote on it at the dictation of Jeremiah all the words of the scroll which Jehoiakim king of Judah had burned in the fire; and many similar words were added to them" (36:32). Here we see something of the method of the prophet in recording the revelations which God gave.

Turning again to the reign of Zedekiah and the invasion of Nebuchadnezzar, king of Babylon, we learn in chapters 37-39 of the personal persecution which fell upon Jeremiah the prophet during the closing days of Judah's national existence. During the siege, Jeremiah left Jerusalem to go to his native Benjamin, but was arrested as a deserter, was beaten and imprisoned in the house of the secretary to the king. When Zedekiah secretly questioned him about a word from the Lord, Jeremiah

stoutly refused to change his message but insisted that the
city would fall into the hands of the king of Babylon.
Though the king meant only to confine him to the court of
the guards, the prophet's enemies within the royal court
conspired against him and he was taken and cast into a
dark cistern partly filled with muck and water. But an
Ethiopian eunuch in the king's court took pity on the
prophet and arranged for his release from the terrible
dungeon. Again with remarkable boldness the prophet
said to King Zedekiah: "Thus says the Lord, the God of
hosts, the God of Israel, if you will surrender to the
princes of the king of Babylon, then your life shall be
spared, and this city shall not be burned with fire, and you
and your house shall live. But if you do not surrender to
the princes of the king of Babylon, then this city shall be
given into the hand of the Chaldeans, and they shall burn
it with fire, and you shall not escape from their hand"
(38:17,18).

The king attempted to evade these words and escape
from the city by night, but in accordance with the prophetic word he was captured by the armies of Babylon and
taken before Nebuchadnezzar; there his eyes were put out
and he was bound in fetters and carried to Babylon. The
walls of the city of Jerusalem were breached and, as
Jeremiah had long been warning, the Babylonians came
into the Temple and the city and carried away all the
treasures of Judah to Babylon, leaving only a remnant of
the people in the land.

Prophecies to the Remnant

After the fall of the city, Jeremiah continued to minister to the remnant of Judah under the governorship of
Gedaliah who had been left in charge of the country by
Nebuchadnezzar. When Gedaliah was murdered by certain of his enemies in Jerusalem, the remnant of the nation
thought to flee to Egypt to escape the terrible conditions

then prevailing in Judah. But Jeremiah waited upon the Lord for 10 days and, at the conclusion of this, summoned the leaders of the remnant and told them they were to remain in the land and God would sustain and keep them if they would do so. They were further warned: "If you set your faces to enter Egypt and go to live there, then the sword which you fear shall overtake you there in the land of Egypt; and the famine of which you are afraid shall follow hard after you to Egypt; and there you shall die" (42:15,16).

But the remnant refused the divine warning and fled to Egypt, taking Jeremiah captive with them. There Jeremiah continued his prophetic ministry, predicting the conquest of Egypt by Nebuchadnezzar, and warning the Jewish fugitives that they must learn from the lessons of history not to persist in idolatry, for God would afflict them in Egypt as He afflicted their fathers in Jerusalem. This too was rejected, and soon Jeremiah's prophecy was fulfilled; for in 568 B.C. Nebuchadnezzar invaded Egypt and carried out the divine word.

The short chapter 45 is a personal word of both warning and encouragement to Baruch the servant of Jeremiah not to seek for himself great things in the midst of God's judgments on the world at that moment in history. It was a wise warning to take note of the movements of God and adjust his personal life accordingly.

Judgment of Surrounding Nations

Chapters 46-51 record Jeremiah's prophetic messages to the nations surrounding Jerusalem. His call was to be a prophet to the nations, and this closing section of his prophecy fulfills that calling. Words of warning and coming judgment are given, first to Egypt (46:2-28) then against Philistia (47:1-7) and Moab (48:1-47) and Ammon, the sister nation of Moab (49:1-6), Edom (49:7-22), Damascus (49:23-27), Kedar, one of the Arabian tribes (49:28,29), and Hazor, a city in the north of Israel which was a confederate of the Arabian tribes (49:30-33).

Then the prophetic vision enlarges and includes Elam (present-day Iraq) where the Tigris River flows. Finally the vision of the nations ends with the description of the fall of Babylon and God's judgment upon them for their cruelty and evil.

Though these prophetic judgments have long since been fulfilled in history, they constitute a present-day word of help to believers when viewed from their typological significance. Each of these ancient nations is consistently used throughout the Old Testament as picturing aspects of what the New Testament calls "the flesh." Here in these nations is pictured characteristics of the fallen nature which we all inherited from Adam. Pride, lust, envy, jealousy, ambition, anger, bitterness, violence, debauchery—all these are faithfully pictured in these enemy nations of Israel, and God's judgments upon them as well.

Review of Jerusalem's Fall

Chapter 52, the closing chapter of the book, is a historical review of the fall of Jerusalem. Its lesson is clear. Although God is a God of marvelous patience and waits until the last possible moment for human repentance, pleading in a hundred different ways for the return of His wandering people, yet inevitably if sin persists there will come a "fifth month, on the tenth day of the month" (see v. 12) when God's word will be carried out to the very letter and no human maneuvering can possibly evade it. When Nebuchadnezzar entered the city of Jerusalem, as predicted, "He burned the house of the Lord, and the king's house and all the houses of Jerusalem; every great house he burned down. And all the army of the Chaldeans, who were with the captain of the guard, broke down all the walls round about Jerusalem" (52:13,14).

The book closes with a brief word concerning God's

grace to King Jehoiachin who had been imprisoned in
Babylon for 37 years. At the end of that time he was taken
from prison and allowed to dine regularly at the king's
table. Thus the great prophecy of Jeremiah ends. The
prophet himself has died a nameless death in Egypt, in
exile, but his words ring through the centuries since as a
faithful recorder of the divine foreview of history and the
certainty of God's purposes in human affairs.

LAMENTATIONS

This little book is an eloquent expression of the sorrow of Jeremiah as he saw his own prophecies fulfilled in
the desolation and destruction of the city of Jerusalem
under Nebuchadnezzar. The Septuagint states that he sat
weeping over the city and lamenting over Jerusalem in
these moving words. The five poems which make up this
book and correspond with its five chapters express not
only the horror and desolations which came upon Jerusalem, but also the anguish of spirit which the prophet
himself felt when these desolations occurred. There is no
exultation over the fulfillment of his predictions, but a
poignant expression of heart misery over the sins of the
people of Judah and their consequent punishment. In this
sense again Jeremiah becomes a type of Christ, the "man
of sorrows, and acquainted with grief" (Isa. 53:3).

The first four chapters are in the form of acrostic
poems, as each verse begins with a letter of the Hebrew
alphabet. The third chapter contains 66 verses, devoting
three verses to each of the 22 letters of the Hebrew
alphabet. Chapter 5, though a 22-verse poem, does not
follow that acrostic form.

In the first poem there are two clearly defined movements. Using the figure of a widow sitting desolate in the

midst of her degradation, the prophet describes Jerusalem as weeping bitterly in the midst of her lovers, finding no one to comfort her. The prophet acknowledges that the desolation has been brought about by the grievous sins of the city. He clearly acknowledges that "the Lord has made her suffer for the multitude of her transgressions; her children have gone away, captives before the foe" (1:5).

The latter part of the poem is an appeal to the passers-by to understand something of the sense of desolation and sorrow which grips the city. Even though it is acknowledged that the siege is well-deserved, appeal is made to the Lord for mercy in a time of great distress.

In the second poem an explanation is given of the sources of the nation's evil. Judgment from the Lord has fallen upon the princes of Israel because of their perfidy. Both king and priest have contributed to the downfall of the nation. Likewise the place of worship has been destroyed and all of Israel's solemn assemblies are degraded. The prophets are judged because of their false visions and prophecies. All comfort is removed from the stricken city because it ignored the faithful warnings of the Lord. Earnest appeal is made, however, to cry to the Lord for deliverance and for His restoring mercy.

Chapter 3 centers upon the feelings of the prophet himself and his identification with the sins and sorrows of the nation. He has fully shared the grief of the people, and has felt in himself the horror of judgment, yet he clearly recognizes that the steadfast love of the Lord has never ceased, and even in the midst of His judgments His mercies are fresh and new.

Jeremiah reminds himself and he reminds the people that the Lord will not cast off forever, nor does He willingly afflict or grieve the sons of men, but will extend mercy and restoring grace when they call and return to Him. The poem ends with the realization that the enemy who brought such desolation upon the city will himself be judged for his evil, and the tender compassion of the Lord will be visible even in the midst of His judgments.

Chapter 4 is a dirge of desolation, describing again the disasters which befell Jerusalem because of its sin, which the prophet describes as greater than that of Sodom. The blame for all this is largely laid at the feet of the prophets and priests within the city who utterly failed to discharge their ministry. It ends with a satirical address to the nation of Edom to beware for it too shall come under Jehovah's judging hand.

The final poem is an appeal from a sorrowing heart to a merciful Lord to restore the nation. The prophet recognizes that the people cannot turn to Jehovah apart from His help, and he cries in helplessness: "Restore us to thyself, O Lord, that we may be restored! Renew our days as of old!" (5:21).

In its application to the individual, the book of Lamentations may be taken as a parallel expression of Psalm 51, which is the cry of a heart that has become aware of its deserved punishment, yet casts itself upon the mercy of God as its only hope in the hour of affliction. It is a recognition that though grief has been brought by the righteous hand of God, it is the loving heart of God which can be appealed to for restoration.

CHAPTER SEVEN

God Rules

EZEKIEL

The two prophecies of Ezekiel and Daniel are found back to back in our English Bibles, and the men who wrote these prophecies were contemporaries during the days of the exile of Judah and Israel. Ezekiel, the older of the two, was carried to Babylon by Nebuchadnezzar after his first invasion of the land of Judah, when King Jehoiachin was taken captive. Ezekiel was a young man of 25 at the time, on his way to becoming a priest when he reached the required age of thirty. His apprenticeship was rudely interrupted by the siege of Jerusalem and his consequent capture and exile.

Daniel likewise was carried to Babylon when but a young man. He was of the royal line of Israel and recognized as a promising young prince of the royal family. He too was taken to Babylon by Nebuchadnezzar, but in another group from that of Ezekiel. Doubtless the two young men knew each other, although no record is given in Scripture of their acquaintanceship. In one reference Ezekiel does refer to Daniel, along with Noah and Job, but otherwise the record is silent about what must have been a continuing friendship between them.

There is no question but what Ezekiel is the most

colorful and unpredictable of the prophets. One writer calls him "the wildest man in the Bible." To this unusual young man is granted weird and wonderful visions of the majesty and mystery of God; nothing of a similar nature is found anywhere else in the Bible. He is shown the glory of the Lord in such cosmic proportions that language fails to describe it accurately, and he resorts to strange and even bizarre symbolism to depict what he sees. Further he is given strange assignments by the Lord to act out, in bizarre fashion, the messages he is asked to convey to the people.

Though his prophecy is written in Babylon, by means of visions and trances he returns frequently to Jerusalem and describes much of what is happening in the hidden areas of the Temple in that city. The message, therefore, is addressed not only to the exiles in Babylon, but includes also much direct exhortation to the Jews who remained in the land of Judah. Without a doubt he is one of the most gifted and effective communicators of unpleasant truth to be found among the prophets.

Lamentations, Warnings and Woe

The prophecy opens dramatically with a shattering vision of the glory of God, seen amidst the desolate surroundings of the refugee camp of Jews, beside the Grand Canal which is called the River Chebar. The vision came from the north and took shape as a great fiery burning cloud from the midst of which emerged, first, four strange living creatures, each with four faces and four wings. The four faces were those of a man, a lion, an ox, and an eagle. This detail seems to parallel the vision of John in the book of Revelation, chapter 4, where he saw four living creatures before the throne of God; the first like a lion, the second like an ox, the third with the face of a man and the fourth like an eagle. It is apparent that these creatures, whatever else they may be, are always connected with the majesty of God and represent qualities in the character of God. The face of a man pictures intelligence and understanding; that of an ox symbolizes servitude and sacrifice; the lion is the king of beasts and stands for sovereignty and supremacy; the eagle is a heavenly creature, and represents transcendent power and omniscient vision.

It has been pointed out by others that the four Gospels present exactly these same qualities in Jesus Christ. He appears first in the Gospel of Matthew as King, like a lion in the kingdom of beasts, sovereign over all. In the Gospel of Mark He is the Servant, the humble and sacrificing ox. In the Gospel of Luke He is the Man, intelligent, insightful, understanding all of life. In the Gospel of John He is clearly represented as Deity, containing in Himself the life of the heavens, and giving it in sovereign grace to all whom He calls.

Further, Ezekiel saw in his amazing vision a strange combination of great cosmic wheels which seemed able to go in all directions at once. This is generally taken to symbolize the processes of the government of God. In the center of the square formed by the living creatures, there was something that burned like coals and flashed like lightning. Perhaps it is not surprising that UFO enthusiasts have seen some justification for describing this as a visit of spacecraft to earth, containing four spacemen whose helmets appeared to Ezekiel as the four faces he describes.

But Ezekiel saw something far greater than the mere visit of non-terrestrials. Seated on the throne which was on the burning platform was one who was the "likeness of the glory of the Lord," wrapped in a rainbow of dazzling and exquisite colors (see 1:26-28). The details given of the living creatures and the great wheels are symbolic expressions of aspects of the Great Being whom Ezekiel saw on the burning platform. The creatures "had the form

of men" (1:5) which suggests the divine desire to work
through humanity as the chosen vessel of God's self-
revelation. Their straight feet speak of stability in the
Lord's work. The burnished color is a reference to purity.
The hands under their wings graphically describe the
practicality which must go with heavenly endeavors.
Their wings suggest mobility, and the covering of their
bodies, modesty. The fact that "each went straight forward" (1:12) indicates great sense of purpose and integrity. Yet they went "wherever the spirit would go" (v. 12),
which describes availability. And their appearance as
lightning speaks of tremendous activity. In all this Ezekiel
was being shown that God moves in the human world
through His created beings, but in such a way that His
service is both demanding, exhilarating and terrifying,
and like nothing else man can ever engage in.

The fact that the great wheels, full of faces, could
move in four directions simultaneously is a vivid description of omnipresence. Their great size and awesome power is descriptive of omnipotence, and their rims full of
eyes pictures divine omniscience. Before this marvelous
vision, Ezekiel fell on his face, fully aware that here was
something far beyond his ability to comprehend and, least
of all, to employ to his own advantage. Thus his prophetic
ministry began, as Isaiah's, with a humbling and yet
energizing vision of the mystery and majesty of God
engaged in His awesome ministry in the world.

Though Ezekiel seems to be shattered by the vision of
the glory of the Lord, he is not left to lie on his face in the
dust of the ground. He heard a voice speaking to him,
addressing him as "Son of man" (2:1), and commanding
him to stand upon his feet, and when he did so he felt the
Spirit entering into him and the commission was given to
him to minister to the people of Israel, regardless of
whether or not they would receive his word.

Suddenly as Ezekiel stands there, a hand appears out

of nowhere, holding a scroll with writing on both the front and back. The words written were described as "lamentations and mourning and woe" (2:10). To the young prophet, who must have been unnerved by all he had seen thus far, the command is given: "Son of man, eat what is offered to you; eat this scroll, and go, speak to the house of Israel" (3:1). In obedience, Ezekiel opened his mouth and ate the scroll and found it was in his mouth as sweet as honey. The Lord was impressing upon Ezekiel the fact that assimilation of the divine Word may appear unpalatable and even repulsive at first, but when actually obeyed, even the "lamentations, warnings and woes" become sweet to the taste. The prophet must allow the awesome truth of God to sink into his being and permeate his whole humanity so that his will would be nerved by something more than human energy; but the sweetness of God's truth would carry him through the ordeal ahead. He was then clearly told that the people to whom he would go would have hard faces, strong foreheads, rebellious looks and bad attitudes; but he would be made equally strong that he might stand against them.

Then, amidst the whirring of the wheels, the great vision departed and Ezekiel found himself still among the exiles along the River Chebar, where he sat overwhelmed in silence for seven days. Thus the amazing ministry of Ezekiel began, amidst a further warning from Jehovah that he was to be a watchman over the house of Israel and must be faithful to his task at his own peril.

In chapters 4-7 the unique ministry of warning continues in a series of symbolic acts by the prophet. Without speaking audible words, in a series of four charades the prophet describes what is about to happen to Jerusalem. First he draws on a brick a picture of the siege of the city. Then at the command of the Lord he lies upon his left side for 390 days and on his right side for 40 days. Each of the 390 days stands for a year and depicts the length of

Judah's trouble, and the 40 days imply 40 years of punishment which would be visited upon her. The third sign was that of the prophet's own food which was to be nothing but bread and water indicating the famine and desolation which would accompany the destruction of Jerusalem. Finally he took a sword and sharpened it as a razor, cut off his hair and beard and divided it into three parts: the first to be burned, the second to be hacked to pieces with a sword and the third to be scattered to the wind, indicating how a third of the people of Jerusalem should die by siege, another third killed in battle, and the remaining third taken in exile to the four winds of the heavens.

These actions were followed by strong messages of denunciation and exhortation to the people. It was all to the end that they would know that God is God and able to fulfill His divine Word.

Chapters 8-12 are devoted to an extended vision which began as the elders of Israel sat in the prophet's house in Babylon and waited in silence for his prophetic utterance. Suddenly the prophet seems to be caught up by the hair of his head and finds himself transported in vision to Jerusalem. Standing in the court of the Temple, he is permitted to see the hidden idolatries going on in secret places within the Temple conclave, and at the very gate of the altar he is shown the "image of jealousy" (probably a foul sexual symbol which the people of Israel were worshiping) which arouses God to a terrible jealousy.

Next he sees 70 elders worshiping creeping things and loathsome beasts, and the women of the Temple court weeping for the Babylonian deity, Tammuz, the god of vegetation and fertility. Finally, in the inner court of the Temple the prophet saw 25 men, with their backs turned toward the Temple, worshiping the sun.

In response to this corruption, the prophet is charged to call those who had charge of the city to draw near. In response six men immediately appeared, armed with weapons, and a seventh, clothed in linen with a writing case at his side. They were charged to pass through the city and slay the inhabitants, but the man with the inkhorn was to put a mark on the foreheads of those who mourned the abominations which were committed. During this holocaust of destruction the Shekinah glory of God was seen to move from the holy place to the threshold of the Temple, and the cherubim of God's glory again appeared to the prophet as he had seen them by the River Chebar. The man with the inkhorn was commanded to pass between the whirling wheels and gather coals of fire and scatter them over the city. The Shekinah glory then moved from the court of the Temple to a place beyond the eastern gate. By this the prophet is informed that the ultimate catastrophe is to have God withdraw from His people.

Finally the prophet is shown a group of 25 men, led by the princes of Israel, who are plotting revolt against Babylon and declaring that they must free Jerusalem for it is a boiling pot doomed to destruction. Filled with the Spirit, the prophet declares to them that flight will not avail them anything for they will be destroyed at the borders of Israel.

While he was prophesying, one of the princes suddenly died and Ezekiel fell on his face and cried: "Ah Lord God, wilt thou make a full end of the remnant of Israel?" (11:13). In answer a gleam of hope is given him, for God promises the day will come when He will Himself take out the stony heart of flesh from His rebellious people and give them instead a new heart and a new spirit within them. Then the glory of the Lord lifts from the city and rests upon the Mount of Olives to the east, a clear foreview of the day when Jesus of Nazareth, the promised Messiah, would leave the Temple courts, pronouncing judgment upon them, and make his way across the Kidron Valley to the Mount of Olives, from which, after His crucifixion, He would ascend to the glory of the Father.

In chapters 12-14 the prophet again teaches by means of a series of symbolic action interspersed with messages of doom. First he enacts the part of a refugee by carrying only an exile's baggage from his own house. After denouncing the false prophets and prophetesses among them, Ezekiel warns that God will not accept mere lip service for repentance, but judgment cannot be stayed apart from a true turning to Him. Using various parables and metaphors, the prophet describes in stark and bitter words the fate of Israel because of her idolatrous harlotry and her base ingratitude to the God who has tenderly cared for her and loved her. She will be like a harlot stripped, humiliated and destroyed before those to whom she had given herself in wild abandonment. Further warning is given that no escape from judgment can be achieved by reliance upon Egypt or other powers around, nor can any refuge be found in the self-righteous argument that the present generation is suffering for the sins of their forefathers. But like Jeremiah, Ezekiel himself is greatly affected by what he pronounces, and in chapter 19 he utters a beautiful allegorical dirge to mourn the downfall of Israel.

Again the elders of Israel come to the prophet and sit before him, confident that God will preserve His chosen people from harm without judgment. Again, in chapters 20-24, the prophet speaks in the plainest of language to describe the vileness of Israel's sin. Under the figure of two lewd sisters Oholah and Oholibah, representing Samaria the northern kingdom and Judah the southern kingdom, the prophet describes the lust of Israel for pagan idols and the foulness of their worship under terrible terms of harlotry and lewdness. For this, judgment upon the nation is inevitable but in the days of their terror and despoliation the people shall at last know that the Lord is God.

So in chapter 24 the word of the Lord came saying, "The king of Babylon has laid siege to Jerusalem" (v. 2). To illustrate this graphically to the people the prophet is told that the Lord is about to take the delight of his eyes away from him at a single stroke, and yet he was not to mourn or weep or let his tears run down (see v. 16). This was immediately fulfilled for Ezekiel says: "So I spoke to the people in the morning, and at evening my wife died. And on the next morning I did as I was commanded" (v. 18). So also the Temple, the delight of Judah's eye, would be destroyed, and yet the people were not permitted to mourn its overthrow but were carried away into exile to pine away and groan to one another.

Judgments Against Foreign Nations

In chapters 25-32 there is a series of judgments pronounced against foreign nations which are guilty of crimes against the people of God. Since Israel could not sin with impunity, neither could other nations escape the wrath of God. But though this is true, there is also a parallel principle found throughout the Scriptures that the enemies of God cannot overthrow His purpose of redemption and salvation. There will ultimately be a restoration of the people of God and every promise of glowing beauty and prosperity will be fully carried out, not by the wisdom and power of men but by the grace and mercy of God.

Seven nations are thus submitted to the judgment of God. Four of them, Ammon, Moab, Edom and Philistia, are dealt with briefly and quickly. Each of the four gloated over the punishment of Judah and Israel and took advantage of their downfall. For this reason they are to be given over to avenging marauders.

Tyre and Sidon are dealt with at much greater length, especially Tyre. The sin of Tyre is that of godless materialism, but she too finally expresses rejoicing over the downfall of Jerusalem, and her expectation of enrichment from that overthrow. But God will shatter her false security, bringing up many nations against Tyre and reducing her to a barren rock and a village of fishermen. This prophecy was fulfilled with absolute accuracy of detail. The prophet pictured Tyre as a great ship that would be wrecked by the wind and seas, and ultimately sink into oblivion. The prophecy ends with a message directed to the prince of Tyre, who is evidently the reigning king, and a further lamentation against the king of Tyre, who is a supernatural authority of terrible evil, whose instrument the prince of Tyre was. Commentators have rightly seen this as a description of Satan, for the prophet describes his original appointment by God and the nature of his sin, which began when a terrible pride was found in him and murder became his method.

Chapters 29-32 are devoted to a description of the coming overthrow of Egypt as the principle foe of the people of God. The two great superpowers of Ezekiel's day were Babylon and Egypt, and these two giants were continually struggling for dominance. In a series of seven oracles against Egypt, the prophet makes plain that the battle for world dominion would end in disaster for Egypt and even the power of mighty Pharaoh cannot prevent the destruction of Judah nor the scattering of her people among the nations.

In this prophetic series Nebuchadnezzar is named as the instrument of God's judgment on Egypt, "the great dragon of the Nile." Egypt is also depicted as a great cedar, spreading her lofty boughs of influence among the nations, yet the great tree will be cut down and left broken upon the land to the consternation of the people of earth. Thus, finally, Pharaoh, mighty as he is, will join other nations who have lifted themselves in pride and arrogance and shall lie with them among the uncircumcised of the earth in the Pit of Sheol.

For years, Ezekiel's call was to be a predictor of

disaster; but at last in chapters 33-39 he is permitted to become the proclaimer of God's restorative grace.

Renewal and Reunion

Chapter 33 contains the news of the fall of Jerusalem, which came to Ezekiel through a refugee from the city. Before this, Ezekiel is newly commissioned as a watchman to Israel, since he is to begin a new task as the messenger of hope. The limitations on his speech are removed and he prepares to proclaim the message of renewal and even of reunion of the nation. When the exiles saw that his prophecies of the overthrow of Jerusalem had come true he became immediately the sensation of the nation. Curious crowds gathered to hear him, but for the most part their hearts remained untouched by the message of grace. To them the prophet still gives words of warning of God's ultimate judgment.

Then, at the command of the Lord he speaks to the shepherds of Israel, that is, the rulers of the people. They are charged with exploiting the sheep and feeding only themselves. But these false shepherds would be relieved of their duties and replaced by a Good Shepherd. God Himself would come to them and be their Shepherd-King, ruling His people with mercy and justice, providing to the very weakest, refuge and protection.

The fulfillment of this beautiful promise would begin with the gathering of Israel upon its ancient hills in Palestine. The land itself would be restored to productivity and prosperity, and the mountains of Israel would experience the blessing of God, in contrast with the Mount of Seir (Edom) which was still to suffer under the judgment of God. As God had once promised, He would put His Spirit within His people and remove from them their stony hearts and give them a heart of flesh. The fulfillment of these promises began with the restoration of Israel from the exile in Babylon but stretched on through the centuries to follow to the time of the coming of the Messiah, the Good Shepherd, and on through His first appearance to the very end of the age, when at last, after long years of further exile, the nation Israel would be restored to its land in penitence and mourning and would then experience the total fulfillment of God's promise.

To demonstrate how this would be accomplished, Ezekiel is once again seized by the mighty Spirit of the Lord and transported to a valley full of dry bones. Surveying this desolate scene, the prophet must have been startled to hear the Lord say to him: "Prophesy to these bones, and say to them, O dry bones, hear the word of the Lord" (37:4). But when he began to preach to the bones, a remarkable thing occurred: The preached word held such power that the bones began to shake and rattle everywhere in the valley, clicking themselves together until whole skeletons appeared everywhere. While the prophet watched, sinews came upon them and flesh covered them, followed by skin, so that the valley was occupied by corpses, lying perfectly formed yet unliving.

This time Ezekiel is told to preach to the wind, and on doing so the wind blew upon the corpses and they sprang to life, a great living army.

As if this great and amazing sight were not enough to restore hope to the people, the prophet is told to take two sticks, marking one Judah and the other Joseph, standing for the northern kingdom. These he joined together in his hands so that they appeared to be one stick; and when the people inquired what this meant he told them the purpose of God was to reunite them as a single nation. All this would come to pass under the coming great Shepherd that would appear to Israel, and the people shall know: "My dwelling place shall be with them; and I will be their God, and they shall be my people. Then the nations will know that I the Lord sanctify Israel, when my sanctuary is in the midst of them for evermore" (37:27,28).

But all this was not to happen without further tribulation to the people of Israel. Chapters 38 and 39 are given over to a detailed description of an assault from the far north upon the land of Israel after the people have been restored to Palestine. The great enemy who now appears is no longer Babylon, but "Gog, of the land of Magog, the chief prince of Meshech and Tubal" (38:2). Much controversy has raged among the commentators as to the identity of this new enemy. Gesenius, one of the greatest of the Jewish authorities, identifies Gog as Russia, translating the words "chief prince" as more properly "the prince of Rosh" and Meshech and Tubal. Meshech and Tubal have been identified as ancient forms of the names Moscow and Tobolsk. Thus the great enemy of Israel in the last days is identified as Russia and her satellite nations.

The prophet is told to describe the great enemy as coming out of the north against the land of Israel at a time when its people dwell in security. They will be brought upon the mountains of Israel as a great armed horde advancing like a storm covering the land. But though this fearful host seems to threaten the very existence of the restored nation, nevertheless God intervenes in direct combat and the great army is destroyed upon the mountains of Israel by a terrible rain of hailstones, fire and brimstone from heaven. So great will be the slaughter that it will take seven months to cleanse the land and bury the corpses.

This final restoration of Israel to the land is to be accomplished by the pouring out of God's Spirit upon the house of Israel. It will leave them a people dwelling securely, with none to make them afraid, and then shall all the nations know that the Lord their God has not only sent them into exile but brought them again to be a people and a nation once more. The apostle Paul clearly has this picture in mind in his great prediction of the future of Israel in Romans 11.

The closing chapters of Ezekiel's vision 40-48, constitute one of the most dramatic predictions in all the Bible and one which has been a continuing puzzle to the commentators.

The prophet is caught up once again by the Spirit of God and in vision is taken to a high mountain overlooking the city of Jerusalem. Historically, at the time of this vision Jerusalem had been lying in ruins for some 14 years, but in his vision the prophet sees no longer a city in ruins but a city of beauty and order, dominated by a great new Temple which is the center of the worship of God. To aid the prophet in understanding his vision, an angelic being appears with a measuring rod in his hand. Throughout the vision he measures everything that is seen and reports the measurement in precise detail to the prophet. The symbolism of measuring is a way of underscoring the definiteness of the vision as something real and not imaginary, and also its divine ownership as something God will bring about and not man. It is a symbol which is used also in Zechariah's prophecies in the Old Testament and John's visions in the book of Revelation in the New Testament.

In chapters 40-42 the prophet is taken on a tour of the outer courts of the Temple and then the inner courts, being shown not only the great altar of sacrifice but the chambers for the priests, the decorations of the holy place and the great courts which surrounded the Temple on all sides. All of this is carefully measured and the measurements noted with precise detail.

Chapter 43 records an event which must have been of great encouragement to Ezekiel's heart, for he records: "And behold, the glory of the God of Israel came from the east; and the sound of his coming was like the sound of many waters; and the earth shone with his glory" (43:2). That cloud of shining Shekinah glory entered the Temple by the eastern gate, and as the prophet watched, the glory came into the Temple and filled the whole Temple.

The chapter continues to describe the worship of the people and the sacrifices which were performed by the priesthood in that day. There are certain noticeable differences from the pattern of sacrifices offered in the Temple of Solomon as well as those offered in the Temple of Herod in our Lord's day. Though the Passover reappears, there is no mention of the Day of Atonement or the Feast of Weeks (Pentecost).

Much controversy has raged over the meaning of these omissions and of the significance of animal sacrifices being again offered after the one sacrifice of Jesus on Calvary. Those who see this vision as entirely symbolical of spiritual realities for the people of God today have no difficulty here, but those who hold to a literal temple to be rebuilt for the millennial kingdom find it somewhat embarrassing to explain these. They may however be viewed as purely memorial in character, much as the Lord's table is to us today.

Following the return of the glory of the Lord to the Temple, the prophet is shown a river of water which flows from underneath the threshold of the Temple toward the east. As it flowed, it deepened and widened in dimension. When the prophet was bidden to enter it, it was ankle deep; then reentering further downstream, it was knee deep; 1,000 cubits further it was deep enough to swim it. As he and the measuring man came back along the bank of the river the prophet saw many trees growing. He was told that wherever the river flowed everything it touched would live. The leaves of the trees were to be used for the healing of the nations, and their fruit would be for the people's food.

Finally he was shown a vision of the entire land of promise itself, divided among the 12 tribes, with the Temple in its midst and a special provision made for the Levites, the priests, and the prince.

The vision closes with the designation of the gates of the city and the simple yet sublime name given to the entire city: *Jehovah Shamah* which means "Jehovah is there."

It is a most wonderful and fitting termination for this marvelous vision of Ezekiel. The prophet had been shown the essential glory of God and the greatness of His majesty, and had also seen, in clearest vision, the vile and reprobate sin of the people of Israel. He had beheld the glory of God departing from the city because of these sins, but had lived to see it, in vision, restored by the grace of God, with the people living in purity, harmony and safety under the arching promise of the words, "The Lord is there" (48:35).

The vexing question of whether Ezekiel's temple is one of literal construction yet to appear in the last days, or merely symbolical representing the realities of the New Covenant experienced by God's people today, has been a question debated for centuries. Certainly no such building has ever appeared in history as of this date. But it is clearly futile to demand an either/or choice between these two views. It is much more likely that, as we have seen before, both are true. Ezekiel's temple is indeed a symbolic picture of the relationship of a living God to His people today, living under the New Covenant with its intimacy of communion and availability of power and blessing.

But it is surely not wrong to see it also as a precise and detailed revelation of a temple which will yet be built in the city of Jerusalem at the time when God fulfills all His great promises to the people of Israel and makes them once again the head of the nations of earth. In that day all that is now experienced by faith in the believing heart shall be visible to the eye of any observer. Then shall Ezekiel's great city of promise be seen as John the Seer saw it in Revelation 21:2: "And I saw the holy city, new Jerusalem, coming down out of heaven from God, prepared as a bride adorned for her husband."

DANIEL

To be a godly teenager is a tough assignment in any period of history. To continue to be a godly teenager when exposed to pressure from a world system committed to pagan philosophy, is to make the assignment infinitely tougher. But to begin as a teenager in such an environment and yet rise to a position of high honor, despite several changes of government and at the frequent risk of life, is to fulfill the toughest assignment of all. Yet that is the story of the book of Daniel.

Like Ezekiel, Daniel was carried captive to the land of Babylon from his native country of Judah in one of the early deportations under Nebuchadnezzar. Daniel and his three friends, Hananiah, Misha-el and Azariah, were royal princes of the tribe of Judah, and are described in the first chapter of Daniel as "youths without blemish, handsome, and skillful in all wisdom, endowed with knowledge, understanding, learning, and competent to serve in the king's palace" (1:4). These splendid young men serve as a continual example to the youth of any age of the possibility of standing true to principle in the midst of great pressure, and of drawing upon the invisible help of God to remain faithful against all odds.

The central figure of the four is Daniel, whose personal history is traced through four changes of dynasty in the first six chapters, and whose visions of remarkable scope and content are given to us in chapters 7-12.

Counselor to Kings

Chapter 1 records the initial test to which the young men were subjected as they were set aside for special training for service in the government of Babylon. They were assigned a three-year course of indoctrination involving a change of names—to indicate their new loyalties—a change of food, and a change of language. They made no objection to the change of names or language, since these were necessary to participate in governmental affairs. But they did object to the change of food, for the diet required foods forbidden to the Jews. Courteously, Daniel asked the prince of the king's eunuchs to permit a 10-day test of vegetables and water, and when this change of diet produced no ill effect, but rather enhanced their health, full permission was granted to abstain from the rich foods the king had ordered for the remainder of their three years of training. At the end when they were presented to the king, they were found to be 10 times better than any of the other young men from Babylon, also in training.

In chapter 2 Daniel is in trouble again. This time not of his own making. He and his three friends became involved in a situation in which their own lives were at stake, but they were innocent victims of something over which they had no control.

The story centers around King Nebuchadnezzar who dreamed a dream which troubled him greatly, but which he could not understand. In the early morning hours he summoned his magicians and counselors and demanded of them that they not only tell him the meaning of the dream but tell him what the dream itself was. Though they objected that this was a most unreasonable demand, Nebuchadnezzar informed them that if they could not comply with his request they would all be hacked to pieces and their homes destroyed.

We would never have known of this ancient incident were it not that the demand the king made included in its scope Daniel and his three friends. When they learned of their danger, Daniel, through the king's captain, Arioch, obtained an interview with Nebuchadnezzar, asking for time to discover and interpret the dream. When his request was granted he went immediately to his friends and the four of them took themselves to prayer, asking God to reveal the information they so desperately needed to know.

That night in a dream the secret was revealed to Daniel, and in gratitude he blessed the God of heaven in a hymn of beauty and wonder. When he was brought into the king's presence he took great care to inform all that it was the God of glory who had given him the interpretation and not his own wisdom.

Daniel then described the great image of a man which the king had seen in his dream. The head was of gold, the breast and arms of silver, the belly and thighs of bronze and the legs were of iron, with its feet partly of iron and partly of clay. As the image stood complete a great stone appeared, cut by no human hands, and fell upon the image's feet and broke the entire image into pieces, which were then blown away by the wind so that no trace could be found. But the stone grew into a great mountain and filled the whole earth.

The prophet then informed the king that he and his kingdom of Babylon was represented by the head of gold. He would be succeeded by another empire, represented by the chest and arms of silver, which history records was the Medo-Persian empire. A third kingdom, represented by the belly and thighs of bronze, would then appear, and this was historically fulfilled in the Greek empire under Alexander the Great and his successors. Then the fourth empire, represented by the legs of iron and the feet of iron and clay, would come into being. Historically, this could be nothing else than the Roman empire which was divided into two segments, the eastern and western empires, symbolized by the two legs of the image; then culminating at last in a 10-kingdom empire, indicated by the 10 toes.

Up to this point most commentators are agreed in

interpretation, but much disagreement arises over the meaning of the 10 toes and the mingling of iron and clay. All commentators agree that the great stone which broke the image in pieces represents the kingdom of Christ and the rule of Christ as King of kings and Lord of lords. However the fulfillment of the dream seems to picture the second coming of Christ rather than the first, so that in some sense the fourth kingdom of the Roman empire is seen to continue in history until the end of the age. Many Bible teachers, therefore, teach that the final form, represented by the 10 toes, will reappear at the close of the age as a 10-nation confederacy under the leadership of the beast of Revelation 13, the final world dictator. Further prophecies in Daniel seem to confirm this interpretation and link closely with the vision seen by John in the book of Revelation.

At any rate, when King Nebuchadnezzar heard Daniel's interpretation he fell upon his face and did homage to Daniel, making him ruler over the whole province of Babylon and appointing his three friends as fellow administrators with him.

In chapter 3 the story reverts to the personal history of the young Israelite men in their attempt to live godly lives in the midst of pagan Babylon. Perhaps in prideful distortion of the identification of Nebuchadnezzar as the head of gold in his dream image, the king erects a great image made wholly of gold and sets it up on the plain of Dura, commanding the worship of the entire people of the land. When Hananiah, Misha-el and Azariah, under their new names of Shadrach, Meshach and Abednego, hear the command of the king they refuse to give homage to the image; when the report of this was brought to Nebuchadnezzar he fell into a great rage. Summoning the young men into his presence, he warned them that if they refused to obey his edict they would be cast into a great, burning fiery furnace and consumed alive. Their answer is a model of courage and faith. They said: "Our God whom we serve is able to deliver us from the burning fiery furnace; and he will deliver us out of your hand, O king. But if not, be it known to you, O king, that we will not serve your gods or worship the golden image which you have set up" (3:17,18).

This is a clear instance of the problem created when the law of the land runs contrary to the command of God. But these young men recognized that no human government has the right to command the worship of any people, and rather than compromise their consciences by some outward conformity, they boldly committed themselves to God, submitted themselves to the punishment which the king devised, and were thrown into a furnace which had been heated seven times hotter than usual.

But in the furnace they found a new freedom, for only their bonds were burned, and when the king looked into it he saw not only the three men he had cast in, but the form of a fourth whom he recognized to be the Son of God. Thus, in the words of Hebrews 11 "through faith they quenched the violence of fire" (see Heb. 11:33-34), and gave continual encouragement to all those who, like they, are called to live in a secular and sensuous age which is able to bring great pressure to conform upon those who seek to walk with God. The threat of losing popularity, money, friends or position is often like a fiery furnace which we fear to face, but if we truly believe the unseen God who is able to deliver, we too can count on Him to bring us safely through the fires of persecution and pressure to a greater position of honor and influence, as these young men experienced.

The opening chapters of Daniel are clearly the story of how one brave and godly young man with his three companions so influenced the mightiest king then on earth that the king ultimately became a humble believer in God himself. This story is completed in chapter 4, which

opens with the edict of King Nebuchadnezzar to all the
peoples, nations, and languages of the earth to worship
the most high God whom he has discovered. He then
gives in detail the account of how his great pride was
humbled and he was brought at last to faith in the living
God.

Again it began with a dream which alarmed him and
which he called his astrologers and magicians to interpret.
But once again it is Daniel (who here is called by his
Babylonian name, Belteshazzar) who gives the interpretation. This time the king told the prophet what he had seen.
He had seen a great tree growing in the midst of the earth
whose top reached the heavens, but by angelic power it
had been cut down and stripped of its leaves and fruit,
with only its stump left in the earth until seven years had
passed.

Because Daniel immediately saw the interpretation of
the dream as it applied to the king, he was reluctant to give
the interpretation, but in loyalty to the truth he informed
the king courteously that the king was the great tree and
that he would be removed from his throne and driven out
from among men to live among the beasts of the field,
eating grass like an ox, until the seven years had ended.
Daniel then urged the king to break off his sins and
practice mercy and righteousness that the sentence might
at least be delayed.

But at the end of one year, as Nebuchadnezzar gloated
in pride over the beauty and greatness of Babylon which
he felt he had made, he was suddenly seized with mental
cloudiness and lost his reason so that he was indeed driven
out from men, living as an animal in the fields. When his
reason at last returned, Nebuchadnezzar recognized the
God of heaven and upon being restored to his kingdom he
praised God who was able to humble the proudest of men.

The next scene, in chapter 5, occurs in the reign of
Nebuchadnezzar's successor, Belshazzar. This man who

for a long time was not known to history has now been discovered to be the grandson-in-law of Nebuchadnezzar; he was made a co-regent for a portion of the empire of Babylon.

On the occasion of the annual feast of the gods, Belshazzar invited a thousand of his lords and their wives and concubines to the palace. At this time the city was under siege by Cyrus, the Persian emperor, whose attacking army was led by one called Darius the Mede. The licentious feast of King Belshazzar reached its height when he called for the golden vessels taken from the Temple in Jerusalem and the king and his guests drank wine from the vessels, praising their pagan gods in deliberate blasphemy of the God of Israel. Immediately a supernatural hand appeared and wrote upon the plaster of the wall certain Persian words. As in the reign of his grandfather, the wise men of the kingdom were unable to interpret the meaning and Daniel, by now an old man, was called in. With boldness he rebuked the king for his licentious ways and his persistent refusal to recognize the true God, and interpreted the writing as indicating that God had numbered his kingdom, weighed it as to its value and determined to divide it among the Persians.

That very night, as history records, two Babylonian deserters led Persian invaders under the wall of the city where the Euphrates River had been diverted, and the defending garrison found itself attacked from within. That same night the king was slain as the Persian troops raged through the city.

Chapter 6 is one of the most famous stories in the Bible. It is the story of Daniel in the lions' den. Darius the Mede reorganized the government of Babylon and made all the executives responsible to three presidents, of whom Daniel was one. His wisdom and judgment were so superior that the king planned to set him over the entire kingdom, but this aroused a spirit of jealousy among the other presidents and satraps. They cunningly plotted Daniel's downfall by inducing the king to sign a decree that for a period of 30 days no one should petition either God or man, save the king. Flattered by this, Darius signed the decree, making it the law of the Medes and Persians which could not be changed.

When Daniel heard of it he continued his daily act of prayer, kneeling openly before the windows which opened toward Jerusalem. Reluctantly the king was forced to commit Daniel to the den of lions, but it was the king who spent a sleepless night. It is ironic to see how royally the prophet was kept. The king of beasts stood guard over him. The king of Persia sat up all night out of concern for him, and the King of kings sent His angel to protect him. When Darius found Daniel safe the next morning he issued a great proclamation glorifying the God of Daniel for His power and majesty.

Prophet of the Last Days

Chapters 7 through 12 chronologically revert to the realm of Belshazzar, and the visions which Daniel received under his reign, and carry us forward to the reign of Cyrus the Persian and the revelations which came to the prophet during those days. Though it is not apparent to an English reader, there is another link which ties chapter 7 to chapter 2. The whole portion of the prophecy between these two boundaries appears in the Aramaic language rather than Hebrew. Aramaic was the language of Babylon, a Gentile language. Thus the section fittingly begins with a vision tracing the entire course of Gentile supremacy in the world; for Nebuchadnezzar's great dream image of chapter 2 covers the same general course of history as Daniel's vision of four beasts, found in chapter 7. There Daniel is shown a vision of four great beasts arising out of the Mediterranean Sea. The first was like a lion, the second like a bear, the third like a leopard and the fourth was a great and terrible animal with great iron teeth, different from all the preceding beasts. It had 10 horns and as the prophet watched, three of the first horns were plucked up by an eleventh horn which grew up among them, having the eyes of a man and a mouth speaking great things.

Immediately the vision changed and Daniel saw the throne of God and one seated upon it, before whom a stream of fire issued and thousands upon thousands of angels served Him. As he watched, one called the Ancient of Days (who is also described as Son of Man) was presented before Him and to Him was given dominion and glory over all the nations of the earth (see 7:13, 14).

The interpreting angel then announced that the four great beasts were four kingdoms which would arise out of the earth. These seem to be identical with the four kingdoms of the great dream image of Nebuchadnezzar in chapter 2. There the kingdoms are viewed from man's point of view as of great but decreasing value, represented by the gold and silver and the bronze and iron. Here they appear from the divine point of view as great snarling animals fighting and clashing with one another; but most interpreters agree that they represent the same kingdoms, those of Babylon, Medo-Persia, Greece and Rome. The 10 horns which appeared on the fourth beast's head apparently link with the 10 toes of the fourth kingdom in the dream image. The eleventh horn, with the eyes and mouth that spoke great things, is often linked with the great beast of Revelation 13 who appears as the world dictator of the last days and is known as the Antichrist.

Again it is made evident that all these shall fall before the might and majesty of the Son of Man who sits in judgment over the nations of earth and whose kingdom shall ultimately fill the entire earth.

Two years later, still in the reign of King Belshazzar, Daniel sees another vision, this time of two beasts. One is a ram with two horns which pushes to the west, the north and the south. While he watches a he-goat attacks the ram and overcomes him. From the one great horn on the goat grow four horns and from one of these comes forth a little horn which grows exceedingly great and attacks the Temple, eventually taking away the continual burnt offering and desecrating the sanctuary for a permitted total of 2,300 evening and morning sacrifices.

The interpreting angel Gabriel was sent to make the meaning clear. Daniel was informed that the ram was the kingdom of Medo-Persia while the he-goat was Greece with its notable horn standing for Alexander and his rapid conquests. Four kingdoms would arise after him, which history knew as Macedonia, Thrace, Syria and Egypt. The little horn which would grow from one of these was historically the Syrian king named Antiochus Epiphanes. He fulfilled the vision by attacking Jerusalem, entering the Temple and desecrating it by sprinkling the broth of a sow throughout the area, and erecting an image of Jupiter in the holy place. The Temple remained desolated for a little over three years, which is exactly the amount of time during which ordinarily 2,300 morning and evening sacrifices would have been offered. History records that at the end of that time the Maccabean revolt restored the sanctuary to its original function and Syrian power over Jerusalem was ended.

However, many interpreters believe that at Daniel 8:23, which begins "and at the latter end of their rule," the vision leaps over the centuries to the end of the age when a second desecration of the Temple will take place under the leadership of an individual who appears in Revelation 13 as the second beast, the false prophet. It is this desecration to which Jesus refers in Matthew 24 when He speaks of "the abomination of desolation which was spoken of through Daniel the prophet, standing in the holy place" (Matt. 24:15, *NASB*). Daniel is told by Gabriel that the vision "pertains to the appointed time of the end" (Dan. 8:19) and though the two beasts he saw are clearly identified to him, he records that he was "appalled by the vision and did not understand it" (v. 27). Evidently this indicates that there were aspects of the vision which went beyond what the angel had identified for him.

Chapter 9 records what many consider to be the most important prophetic passage in all the Bible; for in the great prophecy of 70 weeks the prophet Daniel is given by God Himself an outline of history from his own day until the end of the age, when the kingdom of the Messiah shall be set up over all the earth.

The vision began while Daniel was praying before God for the return of the people from Babylon to Israel, having been convinced by the prophecies of Jeremiah that the 70 years of exile were about to end. His prayer of confession and supplication is a moving and marvelous recognition of the majesty and faithfulness of God and the helplessness and weakness of man.

In the midst of it, while he was praying and confessing his sins and the sins of his people, the angel Gabriel, appearing as a man, was again sent to him, addressing him as "O Daniel, greatly beloved." He unfolded to him the divine calendar of prophetic events.

Seventy weeks of years were marked out, during which the people of Israel and the holy city of Jerusalem would be brought at last to full salvation and redemption. The word rendered "weeks" really means a period divided into seven. Dr. D. Douglas Young well reminds us that it is definitely misleading to study this Scripture with conventional methods of measuring time. As he put it: "We do better to think in terms of seventy periods of time, each of which is divided into seven parts." The prophet is told that the 490 years (70 times 7) would be divided into three parts. One part, of 49 years duration; a second period of 434 years, to total 483 years; and the third of 7 years only.

By the end of this entire period a six-fold program would have been accomplished: (1) the finishing of transgression; (2) putting an end to sin; (3) the making of atonement for iniquity; (4) the bringing in of everlasting righteousness; (5) the sealing up of visions and prophecy; (6) the anointing of a most holy place.

Looking back from our vantage point in history it is easy to see that the first three were accomplished by the crucifixion and resurrection of Jesus, while the last three remain yet to be fulfilled at the second appearing of Christ.

Daniel was further told that during the first period of 49 years the city of Jerusalem would be built amidst great difficulty. The period would begin with a decree to restore and build Jerusalem, which seems to be the one referred to in Nehemiah and dates at 445 B.C.

The second period of 62 weeks of years, or 434 years, would be terminated when the "anointed one shall be cut off and shall have nothing, and the people of the prince who is to come shall destroy the city and the sanctuary" (9:26). The Anointed One is clearly the Messiah who was indeed cut off by crucifixion at the appointed time, and subsequently the city of Jerusalem was destroyed by the Romans in A.D. 70 and the Temple burned and flattened. Since this was to come "after the sixty-two weeks" it would fall in an unspecified period of time between the 62 weeks and the beginning of the seventieth week which was scheduled to last for seven years.

Most Bible teachers therefore believe the seventieth week is yet future, and will be the same period of time referred to by Jesus as the "great tribulation" (Matt. 24:21). Daniel is told that "the prince who is to come . . . shall make a strong covenant" with Israel for one week of seven years (9:26,27), but in the midst of it shall break his word and defile the sanctuary much as Antiochus Epiphanes did in 168 B.C. Many link this with the apostle

Paul's prediction in 2 Thessalonians 2 of the appearance of a man of sin who shall exalt himself as God and shall appear in the Temple at Jerusalem, proclaiming himself to be God.

The final vision given to the prophet Daniel occupies chapters 10-12. Once again Daniel and certain of his companions were fasting and mourning for a period of three weeks. Suddenly, as with his contemporary Ezekiel, Daniel is given a vision of the glory of God and he saw one whose face had the appearance of lightning, his eyes burning like flaming torches and his arms and legs gleaming like burnished bronze, and the sound of his words like a noise of a multitude. The prophet fell into a trance and was awakened by the touch of a hand upon him and a voice addressing him. Evidently again it was the voice of Gabriel sent to interpret the vision for him.

In chapter 11 the angel gives to Daniel a long and intricate series of predicted events which would befall the people of Israel after Daniel's death. Many details were clearly predicted, and history records their fulfillment in the struggles between the Selucid empire of Syria and the Ptolemaic empire of Egypt. After a long succession of battles and military forays, the struggle eventuates in the appearance of Antiochus Epiphanes, whose history begins with verse 21 and carries through verse 35. The details of his conflict with Egypt are clearly given and were as clearly fulfilled, and further prediction is made concerning the profaning of the Temple in Jerusalem, the taking away of the continual burnt offering, and the setting up of the abomination that makes desolate.

Beginning at verse 36, however, a personage identified merely as "the king" is introduced, who is said to "magnify himself above every god, and shall speak astonishing things against the God of gods." Many Bible scholars feel that this clearly identifies him with the predicted man of sin of whom Paul speaks, as well as with the second beast of Revelation 13, of whom John speaks. Daniel is told that at the time of the end the king of the south (Egypt) shall attack him, but the king of the north (Syria and possibly Russia) shall come rushing down upon him with a great army, and tens of thousands shall fall. This seems to identify itself with the invasion of Gog and Magog described by Ezekiel in chapters 38 and 39, and that identification is confirmed by the information given to Daniel that "he [the king of the north] shall pitch his palatial tents between the sea and the glorious holy mountain; yet he shall come to his end, with none to help him" (v. 45). This apparently describes the divine destruction which comes upon the invading northern armies by the great rain of hail and brimstone from heaven, which Ezekiel describes.

The vision continues in chapter 12 with the information that at that time Michael, the great prince who is identified with Israel, shall arise and Israel will be subjected to a time of trouble such as has never been since there was a nation until that time. This phrasing is apparently parallel to that used by Jesus when He refers to the Great Tribulation in these words: "For then there will be great tribulation, such as has not been from the beginning of the world until now, no, and never will be" (Matt. 24:21).

Daniel is further told that this will be followed by a great resurrection from the dead, some to everlasting life and some to shame and everlasting contempt. The prophet is then told to seal the book until the time of the end, which shall be identified by many running to and fro and a great increase of knowledge.

In answer to the prophet's request for information on how long it would take to accomplish these wonders, he is given two further periods of 1290 days and 1335 days. Though these are somewhat uncertain in their interpretation, they may refer to the duration of the Tribulation under the rule of the antichrist, and further indicate that those who maintain their faith for the period of persecution will emerge at last into a time of great universal blessing.

So the prophecies of Daniel are brought to a rather abrupt end, having unfolded many events which at our point in history have already been clearly and accurately fulfilled, yet contain many other predicted events which are yet to be brought to pass. No other predictive passages are quite as revealing until, after several centuries, Jesus of Nazareth will sit upon the Mount of Olives with His disciples gathered around Him and unfold in amazing detail the coming history of the troubled city and its ultimate fate, at the end of the age.

CHAPTER EIGHT

God Persists

HOSEA

In many ways the book of Hosea is the most beautiful book in the Old Testament. It is a love story—the story of a broken marriage and of the heartache which unfaithfulness brings into a life. Yet it is also the story of the persistence of God in fulfilling His promise of redemptive action. It pictures the New Testament promise of Philippians 1:6: "He who began a good work in you will bring it to completion at the day of Jesus Christ."

We are informed in the opening verse that Hosea ministered in the days of Uzziah, Jotham, Ahaz, and Hezekiah, the kings of Judah, and during the reign of Jeroboam, the son of Joash, king of Israel. This would make him a contemporary of Isaiah, Amos, and Micah. It was a time of spiritual declension within the nation and the people were paying lip service to the worship of God, but their hearts were far from Him. It was a case with them as it is often with us that the spirit was willing but the flesh was ready for the weekend!

Chapter 1 opens with the remarkable command of God to the prophet to go and marry a girl who would ultimately prove to be a harlot, and thus to illustrate through the personal history of Hosea the heartbreak of

God when He saw the people of Israel given over to spiritual harlotry. There is no reason to believe that Gomer, the daughter of Diblaim whom Hosea married, was a harlot at the time of their marriage, but it is clear that Hosea was told by God that this would ultimately come to pass. You can't read the prophecy of Hosea without seeing that he loved Gomer with all his heart and at first they must have been wonderfully happy together. When their first child, a boy, was born, Hosea went to God to determine the name for the lad. To his great surprise, God picked the name *Jezreel*, which meant "castaway" and was a name of shame in Israel. It recalled the story of Queen Jezebel and King Ahab who cheated their neighbor Naboth of his vineyard. Their treachery was avenged by the king's general, Jehu, who usurped the throne and ordered the servants to throw Jezebel out the window. Her blood was licked up by the dogs in the courtyard, and the courtyard was named Jezreel, for it was there that Queen Jezebel was cast away (see 2 Kings 9:30-37).

Obediently, Hosea gave this name to his oldest son for he understood that God was thus warning the people that they, too, would be cast away if they didn't recognize the folly of their actions. In the course of time another child, a daughter, was born to Hosea and Gomer. This one was named *Lo-ruhamah*, which means "not pitied." It meant that God would no longer have pity on His people if they continued their stubborn rebellion, for His patience was wearing thin. When this little girl was weaned, Gomer conceived again and bore a third child, another little boy. This one God named *Lo-ammi*, "not my people," for God was saying, "You are not my people and I am not your God" (1:9). Yet in the face of this clear revelation of coming judgment, the prophet was sent also to tell the people that there would come a day when Israel would be restored and their names of reproach taken away and they would be called by all "Sons of the living God" (v. 10).

In chapter 2, though no direct mention is made of Gomer's unfaithfulness, it is clear from the prophet's words that he is feeling great personal anguish over her harlotry. Though Hosea still warns of judgment to come and the fact that God would send the Assyrians raging across the land, he no longer announced this with thunder in his voice. Rather he spoke with tears, and tenderly described the day when love would at last triumph after the bitter lesson of disobedience was learned. He predicted Israel would yet turn back to the God who had loved her so faithfully, and instead of being called "not pitied," Israel would be pitied, and instead of "not my people," they would be named "my people" again.

The five short verses of chapter 3 describe how the prophet was sent to find his wandering wife and bring her back into his home again. Evidently her current husband had tired of her and she was to be sold as a slave, so Hosea went to the marketplace and watched as Gomer was brought up and placed on the dock. She was stripped of all her clothing and stood naked before the crowd. The bidding began, and ultimately Hosea offered 15 pieces of silver and a bushel of barley. The auctioneer's gavel fell, and Hosea had his wife back again.

As he put her clothes on her and led her away, he spoke to her what is perhaps the most beautiful verse in all the Bible: "You must dwell as mine for many days; you shall not play the harlot, or belong to another man; so will I also be to you" (3:3). That this painful but beautiful action was symbolic as a message to the people is made clear in the next two verses: "For the children of Israel shall dwell many days without king or prince, without sacrifice or pillar, without ephod or teraphim. Afterward the children of Israel shall return and seek the Lord their God, and David their king; and they shall come in fear to the Lord and to his goodness in the latter days" (3:4,5). This prophecy seems to encompass both the return from exile in Babylon and the later dispersion among the nations of the world following the destruction of the Temple in A.D. 70, with an ultimate return in penitence and faith at the end of the age in view.

In chapters 4 and 5 the prophet summons the people to hear the Lord's controversy against the inhabitants of the land. Their sin is described in clear detail: "There is swearing, lying, killing, stealing, and committing adultery; they break all bounds and murder follows murder" (4:2). Such open sin is declared to be a result of their religious ignorance and lack of knowledge. Priest and prophet alike are guilty of greed and iniquity, and so the land suffers and the people are subjected to invading hosts.

But in the closing verse of chapter 5 and the opening verses of chapter 6 a clear note of hope is struck, for Jehovah says: "I will return again to my place until they acknowledge their guilt and seek my face, and in their distress they seek me, saying, 'Come, let us return to the Lord; for he has torn, that he may heal us; he has stricken, and he will bind us up. After two days he will revive us; on the third day he will raise us up, that we may live before him. Let us know, let us press on to know the Lord; his going forth is sure as the dawn; he will come to us as the showers, as the spring rains that water the earth' " (5:15—6:3). It is remarkable that here restoration is promised the people "on the third day." Without doubt this has in view the resurrection of Jesus on the third day and the symbol this represents of a new beginning and a new kind of life.

The rest of chapter 6 and all of 7 describe the divine frustration at having tried various ways to reach the people of Israel and awaken them to their peril, yet all to no avail. They were like "a cake not turned" (7:8). That is, undeveloped on one side and burned on the other. Further they were like "a dove, silly and without sense" (v. 11), for they kept calling upon the nations around them for deliverance, only to find themselves trapped and destroyed by the ones to whom they looked for help. Like many today, they kept howling and complaining about their mistreatment, but would not repent and turn to the Lord from whom they might find full deliverance.

In chapters 8 through 10 the prophet employs various figures to describe the coming judgment upon the people and the inevitable invasion from Assyria and exile to that land. They are warned that Assyria is like a vulture over the house of the Lord who shall be permitted to descend upon the people and punish them for their sins. The population of the land will be decimated and the countryside left desolate. Though Israel was once like a luxuriant vine yielding much fruit, the vineyard shall be destroyed and their idols carried away with them to Assyria. Through the prophet, Jehovah speaks with great plainness: "You have plowed iniquity, you have reaped injustice, you have eaten the fruit of lies. Because you have trusted in your chariots and in the multitude of your warriors, therefore the tumult of war shall arise among your people, and all your fortresses shall be destroyed" (10:13,14). Yet it must be remembered that Hosea does not pronounce these words with thunder and lightning, but with deep heart-anguish and an awareness from his own personal history of how Jehovah feels when He visits judgment upon His people.

Chapter 11 opens with the words: "When Israel was a child, I loved him and out of Egypt I called my son. The more I called them, the more they went from me; they kept sacrificing to the Baals, and burning incense to idols." Here again God's loving heart comes bursting through the revelations of judgment as the prophet cries in the name of the Lord: "How can I give you up, O Ephraim! How can I hand you over, O Israel! How can I make you like Admah! How can I treat you like Zeboiim!

My heart recoils within me, my compassion grows warm and tender" (11:8). It is language reminiscent of the scene in the Gospels where Jesus sits on the Mount of Olives and weeps over the rebellious city of Jerusalem.

Yet though God feels the anguish of His people and suffers with them, nevertheless He resolves upon judgment for He knows there is no other way to break the back of the people's rebellion and bring them at last in repentance to His feet. So He declares: "Samaria shall bear her guilt, because she has rebelled against her God; they shall fall by the sword, their little ones shall be dashed in pieces, and their pregnant women ripped open" (13:16).

All through this severe language one can detect a sob in the voice of God as He pronounces judgment. And finally in the last chapter, the love of God comes flashing through the darkness. He cries beseechingly: "Return, O Israel, to the Lord your God, for you have stumbled because of your iniquity. Take with you words and return to the Lord; say to him, 'Take away all iniquity; accept that which is good and we will render the fruit of our lips' " (14:1,2).

To this attitude the divine promise is revealed: "I will heal their faithfulness; I will love them freely, for my anger has turned from them. I will be as the dew to Israel; he shall blossom as the lily, he shall strike root as the poplar; his shoots shall spread out; his beauty shall be like the olive, and his fragrance like Lebanon. They shall return and dwell beneath my shadow, they shall flourish as a garden; they shall blossom as the vine, their fragrance shall be like the wine of Lebanon" (14:4-7).

It should be clear to us as we read this beautiful story that it is really our own personal history. Ours is the blindness that, like Gomer's, cannot distinguish between lust and love. We try to run from God and drown our miseries in empty pleasures or in overwork; but as surely as we think we have escaped, as surely as we think we have run away, God touches our sleeve with His love, saying, "My child, my name and my nature are love, and I must act according to what I am. When you tire of your running and your wandering and your heartbreak, I'll be there to draw you to myself again." At Bethlehem God entered the slave market of this world where the whole human race was putting itself up for auction, prostituting its humanity to a cheapened life. But on the cross the Lord Jesus paid the price of our freedom and bought us back. Thus Hosea is but again the story of God's love and God's heart, revealing His loving desire to make us, His people, the whole persons He intended us to be.

JOEL

For centuries men have been looking for the principle upon which the events of history turned. Since the dawn of history there have been many guesses as to what that principle is. The great Greek philosophers declared that history moves in cycles, and a leading modern historian, Arnold Toynbee, agrees with that. For instance, Aristotle said that history follows a predictable course; first a tyrant rises, a man of iron, who seizes control of a nation and rules until his dynasty ends. Control gradually passes from him to a ruling family of aristocracy, and as their power deteriorates, control passes to the people in what Aristotle called democracy. But the democracy, too, will deteriorate and gradually bring about a breakdown of power until anarchy ensues. Out of anarchy a tyrant again seizes control and so goes the cycle of history.

Other men have felt somewhat differently. Thomas Jefferson thought the hinge of history was political; and when he wrote the Declaration of Independence he incorporated that idea in the prologue, declaring that human governments must recognize certain inalienable rights that are granted to men and, to preserve those rights, governments are instituted among men. He felt, therefore, that the forces that shape human history are political in nature.

In the last century, Karl Marx dipped his pen into the acid of his own embittered spirit and wrote the work that has dramatically influenced our modern time. His idea was that the controlling force of history is economics, and that it is the need to meet the material demands of life that shapes the events of any day. He called this force "dialectical materialism," the principle of material supply arrived at through dialectical discussion, that is, debate. Today millions around the earth feel that economics is indeed the controlling force of life.

H. G. Wells, however, was one of a number of thinkers who said that evolution shapes the course of human destiny. Schools often teach today that behind the events of human history is an evolutionary principle, forcing us on to higher and higher endeavor and making life better and better.

But in many places in the Bible we learn that these insights are all wrong, especially in the book of Joel. Joel declares that the hinge upon which history turns is spiritual—God's Spirit at work among men. Even as early as the great universal flood Noah was told, "My Spirit shall not strive with man forever." In that brief phrase we learn that God's Spirit is in conflict with the spirit of the age, and that the Spirit of God patiently is restraining human evil so that life can go on. But at last God's patience will reach an end and then comes a time—often repeated throughout history—when God removes His Spirit from His restraining ministry and everything collapses, great catastrophes occur, and judgment strikes. It is what the Bible describes as "the day of the Lord." That is essentially the message of the book of Joel.

Joel was a prophet to the kingdom of Judah and also a contemporary of Isaiah, Hosea and Amos. His prophetic vision encompassed not only immediate events of his own day, but as with many of the prophets, he saw to the final stages of God's dealing with human events.

He begins in chapter 1 with a dramatic description of an invasion of locusts upon the land of Judah. As a boy I witnessed such an invasion in Minnesota many years ago. I can still remember how the sky was darkened by the great cloud of insects, and one could hear them descending into the standing grain fields, like hail upon the ground. There was a continual rustling of the noise of their wings as they covered the fields, and within moments every blade of grass, every bit of vegetation was gone, and the fields were left as though they had been plowed.

That is what happened in Israel in Joel's day. A locust horde had descended upon the land and devoured every living thing. The crops were ruined and famine was at hand. Joel calls the attention of the nation to this event, summoning the elders to take heed and even the drunkards to be aware of the disaster that had fallen upon them. His point is that God is behind such an event as this. It is not merely a freak of nature, but happened in obedience to the command of God who works through natural laws to teach His people the lessons they need to learn. Joel clearly implies that if the people will learn this minor-league example of the day of the Lord, they will save themselves the awful heartache that will come in what he later calls "the great and terrible day of the Lord."

In chapter 2 the prophet leaps a great span of time to the end days and uses the invasion of locusts as a picture of the invasion of a great army into the land of Israel in the latter days. He says: "Like blackness there is spread upon the mountains a great and powerful people; their like has never been from old, nor will be again after them through the years of all generations" (2:2). This begins to sound very much like the language Jesus used in describing a time of trouble which would be, He said, "Such as has not been from the beginning of the world until now, no, and never will be" (Matt. 24:21). The prophet describes how the land is scorched behind this great army as it advances, and he describes the army itself as having the appearance of horses. Fear grips the hearts of the people as they see this invading host. "The earth quakes before them, the heavens tremble. The sun and the moon are darkened, and the stars withdraw their shining" (2:10).

Anyone who carefully compares prophetic passages from the Scripture will soon discover there are certain interpretational landmarks. Symbols appear again and again through various books of prophecy so that one can identify the events which are described. The darkening of the sun and the moon, and the withdrawing of light from the stars is one of these landmarks.

Jesus Himself refers to such an event in His great description of the last days in Matthew 24. It appears also in the book of Daniel and in Isaiah and in the book of Revelation. Whenever it is mentioned, it is an interpretational landmark pointing to the last days which mark the coming of the great and terrible day of the Lord.

This section of Joel's prophecy then seems to link directly with the description of the prophet Ezekiel (chaps. 38, 39) of a great northern army which invades the land of Israel, destroying everything before them, and ultimately capturing the city of Jerusalem.

But in each of the prophecies mentioned, God promises that the northern army will be dealt with by direct divine intervention. Isaiah says so, Ezekiel says so, Daniel says so. Now Joel also adds his voice: " 'Yet even now,' says the Lord, 'return to me with all your heart, with fasting, with weeping, and with mourning; and rend your hearts and not your garments.' Return to the Lord, your God, for he is gracious and merciful, slow to anger, and abounding in steadfast love, and repents of evil. Who knows whether he will not turn and repent, and leave a blessing behind him" (2:12-14).

Then the divine promise comes: "I will remove the northerner far from you, and drive him into a parched and desolate land, his front into the eastern sea, and his rear into the western sea; the stench and foul smell of him will rise, for he has done great things" (2:20). Here also the great northern invader is found to be destroyed upon the mountains of Judah. The eastern sea is the Dead Sea and the western sea the Mediterranean, and there, according to both Joel and Ezekiel, the stench and foul smell of decaying corpses will fill the land. And afterward the land itself is called to rejoice and to blossom with fecundity and prosperity. The great promise is: "I will restore to you the years which the swarming locust has eaten, the hopper, the destroyer, and the cutter, my great army which I sent among you. You shall eat in plenty and be satisfied, and praise the name of the Lord your God, who has dealt wondrously with you. And my people shall never again be put to shame" (2:25,26).

This is always God's way of dealing with those who repent and return to Him. I shall never forget the agony in the eyes of a young man who a number of years ago looked at me and said, "You know I've become a Christian and it's wonderful, but when I think back to what I've missed and the years of my life that I've wasted, my heart is sick in remembering it. If I'd only had the sense to come to the Lord before I did all these terrible things." I had the joy of saying to him, "Son, God says 'I will restore to you the years that the locust has eaten.' It is His delight to make up to us for the barrenness of our lives when we return at last to Him."

Beginning with verse 28 on through chapter 3, the prophet describes the means by which God will accomplish His great purposes. Verses 28 and 29 are a familiar and oft-quoted promise: "And it shall come to pass afterward, that I will pour out my spirit on all flesh; your sons and your daughters shall prophesy, your old men shall dream dreams, and your young men shall see visions. Even upon the menservants and maidservants in those days, I will pour out my spirit." Perhaps you will recognize that these are the verses quoted by the apostle Peter when he stood up on the day of Pentecost and, interpreting the sign of tongues of fire and strange languages which the apostles were speaking, he said to the assembled multitudes: "This is that which was spoken by the prophet Joel" (see Acts 2:16-18).

Peter went on quoting from the prophet, pointing out that there would be signs in the heavens when the sun would be turned to darkness and the moon to blood before the terrible day of the Lord shall come. It is clear from this that Joel foresaw both the beginning and the ending of the great period of time which we call now "the age of grace." The pouring out of God's Spirit on the day of Pentecost was to be the initial introduction of an entire age during which there would be no special priesthood or order of prophet, but all God's people would be equipped with spiritual gifts and be enabled to minister one to another.

But that age would end in a time of great universal disaster and the appearance of terrible judgments upon the earth. Those days of judgment will be introduced by a period of intense international warfare, for Joel is told: "I will gather all the nations and bring them down to the valley of Jehoshaphat, and I will enter into judgment with them there, on account of my people and my heritage Israel, because they have scattered them among the nations, and have divided up my land, and have cast lots for my people, and have given a boy for a harlot, and have sold a girl for wine, and have drunk it" (3:2,3). To bring this about, the prophet is told: "Proclaim this among the nations: Prepare war, stir up the mighty men. Let all the men of war draw near, let them come up. Beat your plowshares into swords, and your pruning hooks into spears; let the weak say, 'I am a warrior' " (3:9,10).

Many have quoted the famous words from Micah and Isaiah, "beat your swords into plowshares and your spears into pruning hooks," but little mention is made of this statement from Joel in which the nations are summoned not to make peace, but to make war. It is clear that Joel's prophecy must be fulfilled first and the present course of world events seems to indicate that there is no hope of universal peace until first there must come universal war and divine judgment.

Once again mention is made of the terrible judgments of the great day of the Lord: "Multitudes, multitudes, in the valley of decision! For the day of the Lord is near in the valley of decision. The sun and the moon are darkened, and the stars withdraw their shining" (3:14,15).

But the final scene is one of beauty and glory: "And in that day the mountains shall drip sweet wine, and the hills shall flow with milk, and all the stream beds of Judah shall flow with water; and a fountain shall come forth from the house of the Lord and water the valley of Shittim" (3:18). As we have already seen, this is the way Ezekiel's great vision ends, with a river flowing out from under the threshold of the altar and watering the land. Water in Scripture is a picture of the Holy Spirit and fulfills the word of Jesus in John 7:38: "He who believes in me, as the scripture has said, 'Out of his heart shall flow rivers of living water.' "

It is apparent from Joel that the future is in God's hands and not man's. It is in the hands of One who is preparing something which is beyond anything eye has ever seen or ear has ever heard or has ever entered into the heart of man. God deals with us in judgment that He may capture our attention and wake us up to reality; but through these difficult things God in grace is simply saying: "Adjust your life to reality now that you may be ready for the great things which are yet to come." The promise to Israel is: "But Judah shall be inhabited for ever, and Jerusalem to all generations. I will avenge their blood, and I will not clear the guilty, for the Lord dwells in Zion" (3:20,21). Again, this is where Ezekiel ended his prophecy, with a picture of the restored city under its new name "the Lord is there."

CHAPTER NINE

God Judges

AMOS

The prophecies of Amos and of Obadiah were uttered about a century apart yet their theme is very similar—it is that of the inevitability of judgment when sin is excused and continued. As we've already seen, Amos was a contemporary of prophets such as Isaiah, Joel, Micah, and Hosea. Though he himself grew up in the little town of Tekoa near Bethlehem in Judah, his ministry was largely directed toward the northern kingdom of Israel during the days of Jeroboam II, about the middle of the eighth century B.C. Amos has long been the favorite of social reformers, for his voice speaks with great power and clarity against injustices in social life. He minces no words in describing the atrocities and oppressions which the rich visited against the poor, and in warning the people who lived in comfort and luxury that they were living in a fool's paradise which would soon end in terrible disaster.

The atmosphere of the prophecy of Amos is set in the second verse of the first chapter where the prophet pictures Jehovah as a great lion, roaring out from Jerusalem over the cities of the land, and bringing fear and terror upon the hearts of all who hear the terrible sound.

In chapter 7 the prophet tells us a bit of his personal

history. He was not trained as a prophet, nor even as a priest, but was a common herdsman—a shepherd—and a gatherer of sycamore fruit. From these humble origins he was called by God to utter a prophetic word against the extravagances of the nations surrounding Israel, against Judah the southern kingdom, and primarily against the kingdom of Jeroboam in the north. He is a striking example of the frequent pattern which God follows in calling His spokesman from unexpected backgrounds and without formal training or preparation.

The first two chapters reveal the concern of God for the behavior of nations, especially in the matter of cruelty and oppression. Using the simple formula, "for three transgressions, yea for four" God utters warnings against Damascus, the Philistines, Tyre, Edom, Ammon, Moab, Judah, and an expanded judgment uttered against Israel. The prophetic formula is an indication of patience being pushed to the extreme and finally triggered into action by a sin of such seriousness that judgment can no longer be delayed.

The flagrant sin of Damascus was her barbarous treatment of the northern area of Israel called Gilead. For this, Damascus (Syria) would be ultimately delivered into exile. Gaza (Philistia) was judged for her terrible practice of enslaving peoples and selling them for profit to other countries. Tyre (Phoenicia) was committed to judgment by fire because of her treachery in pursuing the slave traffic at the expense of breaking an agreement she had made with other nations. Edom was doomed because of her unforgiving spirit against related nations around her. Ammon was condemned because of brutality and savagery against Gilead. Moab was to be judged for her violation of the dead. Judah would face ultimate exile because of her ignoring the word of God and her idolatrous practices. All these nations had ignored their moral responsibilities and were to be called into account because of this.

Finally, turning to the northern kingdom of Israel, the prophet described her sins as oppression of the poor, shocking immorality, blasphemy, and open sacrilege which they persisted in despite the fact they had seen the Amorites destroyed for the very sins they were committing. Knowing the concern and care of God for His people as demonstrated in their own history, they had nevertheless given themselves over to open debauchery.

Chapters 3, 4, and 5 all begin with the phrase "hear this word." These three addresses cover chapters 3 through 6 and lay the careful groundwork for the warnings of the prophet and his appeal to the nation for repentance.

The theme of the first discourse, in chapter 3, is that privilege does not preserve from punishment. We often feel, as the nation Israel did, that because we are the special people of God we will be preserved from danger and judgment no matter what we do. By a dramatic series of questions, the prophet points out that when you see certain effects you can be sure of the cause. If you see two people walking together, it is clear they have some agreement. If a lion roars in the forest it is clear he has found some prey. If a bird suddenly falls in its flight it clearly has been taken in a snare, etc. His conclusion is when Jehovah roars like a lion it is time to fear for judgment is near; and when God speaks, then His prophets can only utter what He says.

In the second address, chapter 4, the prophet describes the society women of Samaria as fat cows grown rich and lazy by their indolent lives. They were charged with making excessive demands upon their husbands to satisfy their cravings, and thus contributed to the oppression of the poor and the degradation of the nation.

With stinging irony, Amos invited the peoples to increase their religious practices and to give themselves even more avidly to their rituals and meaningless sacrifices. Since they had chosen to ignore the warnings which

God sent to them in the form of famines, blights, pestilences, and invasions, they may as well give themselves to empty worship since it would afford them the only pleasure they could experience until the judgment would fall.

Beginning his third address, the prophet sang a dirge over the nation as though he were already celebrating its funeral. His words are eloquent, as seen in the exhortation to "seek the Lord and live, lest he break out like fire in the house of Joseph, and it devour, with none to quench it for Bethel, O you who turn justice to wormwood, and cast down righteousness to the earth!" (5:6,7).

Two classes of people were especially singled out for warning. There were those who kept wanting "the day of the Lord." They were the religious hypocrites who made much of their feasts, sacrifices, and solemn assemblies and spoke longingly of the need of God's judgment upon blatant and open sinners, but who were unaware of their own sinful and greedy hearts. To them the prophet declared that God hated their rituals and took no delight in their offerings, and would in no wise spare them from the judgment which was to come.

The second class of people were the indifferent, those who were "at ease in Zion." These were particularly the rulers who had given themselves over to luxury and were living as though no judgment were possible. To them the prophet declared the swift and certain judgments of the Lord, and that they would be the very first to go into exile.

The third division of the prophecy covers chapter 7 through chapter 9, verse 10, and contains five visions which the prophet saw and which symbolized the people's condition. The first was of a plague of locusts which were forming to descend upon and devour the land. But when Amos saw the terrible destruction this would bring about he pled with the Lord to set it aside and his prayer was granted. The second vision was of a devouring fire (perhaps a severe drought) which again portended such destruction that the prophet pled for the people and this judgment was also averted. In the third vision the prophet was shown the Lord standing beside a wall holding a plumb line in His hand. This was a symbol of the deviations of Israel from God's righteous law. By this symbol the prophet learns that God has determined not to restore His people before judgment strikes. Against such terrible finality the prophet falls silent and does not intervene in prayer.

A parenthesis then occurs in which Amaziah, the priest of the false altar at Bethel, sends a lying report to the king concerning the ministry of Amos. With the king's authority behind him, Amaziah ordered Amos to leave the country and in defense Amos pointed out that he had not chosen to be a prophet but God had called him to it and he had no choice but to deliver the message he had been sent to speak. Amos utters a prediction of doom against Amaziah and his family because of his obstinate opposition, and foretells again the exile of Israel in a foreign land.

This interruption over, the prophet resumes his report of his visions describing how he had been shown a basket of summer fruit. Thus the nation was described as overripe and ready for judgment. Once again the prophet describes, in connection with this, the social injustices which had aroused the wrath of God against His people. They enslaved the poor, they cheated those who came to buy wheat, they were dishonest in all their business transactions, and the result would be earthquakes, famines, darkness and utter disaster.

The fifth vision, in the opening words of chapter 9, are a vivid description of the destruction that was to come upon the nation. The prophet saw the Lord Himself standing at the altar in Bethel. Then, in terrible sovereign power, He ordered the land of Israel to be subjected to destruction and the peoples of the nations to come and take them as prey and as exiles to foreign lands.

But, as in the other prophets, the final scene is one of the ultimate restoration of blessing and prosperity. The prophet declares: " 'In that day I will raise up the booth of David that is fallen and repair its breaches, and raise up its ruins, and rebuild it as in the days of old; that they may possess the remnant of Edom and all the nations who are called by my name,' says the Lord who does this" (9:11,12). These words are quoted by the apostle James, in Acts 15, at the great council of Jerusalem, indicating that the prophets had foretold a time when the gospel would go out to the Gentiles as well as to the Jews, and that it would follow the restoration of the Davidic authority. Most commentators feel that this was accomplished in the first coming of Christ as the son of David but would be completely fulfilled in His return.

The closing verses of Amos are a marvelous description of the cleansing of the land and of the people in the final movement of God with Israel. A promise is given: " 'I will plant them upon their land, and they shall never again be plucked up out of the land which I have given them,' says the Lord your God" (9:15).

Thus it becomes clear that even though Amos speaks with severe language and bitter words, the reason for divine judgment is never revenge but only that God may usher in a restored order and bring about an incredible period of blessing and joy.

OBADIAH

The book of Obadiah is the shortest book in the Old Testament and can be read in just a few moments. It seems to be nothing but a pronouncement of doom against the ancient nation of Edom, which has long since disappeared from history and been buried in the dust of the past. Yet the book finds its place in the Word of God, and that fact alone indicates it has a message beyond its immediate fulfillment.

There are several men in the Old Testament named Obadiah, but the prophet who wrote this short prophecy seems to be identified with none of them. The name means "servant of Jehovah" and like a servant this Obadiah keeps himself in the background. He comes quietly onto the stage of prophecy, delivers his message, and is gone.

In Jeremiah 49 there seems to be a quotation from this book and some have surmised therefore that Obadiah was a contemporary of Jeremiah. But it seems much more likely that he prophesied somewhere around the middle of the ninth century B.C. Verses 10 through 14 of the prophecy describe an invasion and capture of the city of Jerusalem. There were four such plunderings of Jerusalem in the history of Judah and the most likely occurrence to link with this prophecy was that which took place under the reign of Jehoram of Judah in about 845 B.C. Obadiah's prophecy is directed toward the southern kingdom of Judah and yet concerns itself wholly with the predicted destruction and downfall of the nation of Edom. This nation, which we have seen frequently referred to in prophetic sections, was a descendant from Jacob's brother Esau. It occupied the rugged mountainous region southeast of Judah, known in Scripture frequently as Mount Seir and whose capital was Sela, which is the Hebrew word for rock. The ruins of the city are known today as Petra, which is the Greek word for rock.

The book of Malachi, the last prophecy of the Old Testament, makes a statement from the mouth of God: "I have loved Jacob but I have hated Esau" (1:2,3). This statement is quoted elsewhere in the Scriptures as declaring a great principle which runs throughout the course of scriptural history. Many have asked why God should make such a sharp distinction between these twin brothers. It is the purpose of the prophecy of Obadiah to answer the question, Why did God hate Esau? The prophecy divides into three parts—verses 1 to 9 revealing the inward attitude of the heart; verses 10 through 14 detailing the outward acts of violence and cruelty charged against Edom; and verses 15 through 21 depicting the ultimate end, both of Edom and of Judah.

The essential evil, which God declares is the source of His unending hatred, is revealed clearly in verse 3, concerning Edom: "The pride of your heart has deceived you, you who live in the clefts of the rock, whose dwelling is high, who say in your heart, 'Who will bring me down to the ground?' " The phrase "you who live in the clefts of the rock" describes the capital of Edom, now known as Petra, which is a valley plateau accessible only through a long narrow ravine, containing within it huge temples carved out of the living rock. The Edomites, therefore, felt themselves to be impregnable. But Obadiah predicts that God will cast down their strongholds and bring them into judgment. Thus the essential evil which is symbolized everywhere in Scripture by Esau and his descendants is that of the pride of self-sufficiency, the philosophy which feels it has no need of God or of any help outside itself.

This inward pride finds its expression in outward acts of violence and cruelty toward Judah, described in verses 10 through 14. When Jerusalem was under attack and the people of Judah were being carried away by strangers who had invaded the city, Edom looked on with delight and shouted for joy at the news of the overthrow of Jerusalem. Furthermore, they took an active part by delivering up the survivors to the enemies of Judah and cutting off those that escaped. Thus for their evil against their brother nation the Edomites stand condemned, and despite their proud self-sufficiency are to be brought low and humbled in the day of the Lord.

Verses 15 through 21 describe the inevitable end of pride. For the prophet states: "As you have done, it shall be done to you, your deeds shall return on your own head" (v. 15). History records that some five years after the fall of Jerusalem, in 586 B.C., the Edomites were forced out of Petra by the Nabataeans, an Arab tribe which was encouraged to the attack by Nebuchadnezzar, and settled ultimately in southern Palestine in an area which the Greeks later called Idumaea. During the Roman conquest of Palestine, the Idumaeans joined the rebellion against the Romans in A.D. 70 and were entirely exterminated during the siege of Jerusalem in the third century A.D. Origen, one of the early church fathers, spoke of them as a people whose name and language had perished.

Obadiah's prophecy closes with a prediction of restoration to come to Judah, here called Mount Zion. Thus is fulfilled the word of Obadiah that "the house of Jacob shall possess their own possessions" and also "there shall be no survivor to the house of Esau; for the Lord has spoken" (vv. 17,18).

The deeper meaning of this little prophecy can only be understood when one sees Jacob and Esau as symbols of the antagonistic principles of the flesh and the spirit in man. God hates Esau and loves Jacob because Jacob stood for all that Esau was not. Jacob represents faith in God and a willingness to submit to God's guidance. Though in the personal life of Jacob there was much of failure and of shame, yet through all his record there shines the glory of faith in God's ability to bless.

But Esau hated that ideal. His own attitude was of self-sufficiency and pride and he took every opportunity to assault his brother Jacob whenever he was down. It has been well stated that every human institution is but the lengthened shadow of its founder, and this principle is seen clearly in the nations of Judah and Edom, which descended from Jacob and Esau. There is a footnote to history in the record of the New Testament which is most remarkable in this regard. In the scenes of Passion Week when Jesus was facing His coming crucifixion, all the Gospels give an account of the time when Jesus of Nazareth stood face to face with King Herod Antipas. Jesus was the son of Jacob, His whole life was lived to express complete and utter faith in God, and in Him was fulfilled the principles of Jacob, but without Jacob's failures and follies. But Herod is an Idumaean, an Edomite, a descendant of Esau. He is proud and arrogant, watching with cruel satisfaction the mockery of the soldiers as they stripped Jesus and dressed Him in robes of royalty. With an evil smile, he plied Jesus with many questions, but for the son of Esau there was no answer from the son of Jacob. He had nothing to say.

The final issue is most remarkable, for the son of Jacob was crucified by the violence of sinful pride but rose a conqueror and is to return to reign as Lord of lords and King of kings, so that, as Obadiah states in his closing words: "the kingdom shall be the Lord's."

But what of Herod, the son of Esau? Tradition tells us that after the crucifixion he returned to Galilee; but soon his pride led him to seek the overthrow of his brother. In appealing his case to the emperor he was dethroned and exiled in Gaul where he died a painful and hideous death. Thus the question which this shortest of the Old Testament prophecies confronts us with is relevant yet today: It is either Jacob or Esau—which do you follow?

As Jesus Himself put it in John 6:63: "It is the spirit that gives life, the flesh is of no avail; the words that I have spoken to you are spirit and life."

CHAPTER TEN

God Waits

JONAH

Probably one of the best known stories in all the Bible is that of Jonah and the fish. Skeptics laugh at the account as one which could not possibly be true, and liberal Bible scholars often regard it as an example of a myth or early legend which was invented to teach a lesson. The book is also known for its reference to Jonah as a jinx or a bad luck person. But all this has obscured the true message of this book. The fact that Jonah was an historical character is confirmed by mention of him in 2 Kings 14:25 where we learn that he lived in Gath-hepher, north of Nazareth in Galilee. Since Jesus referred to him as pre-figuring His own resurrection it is impossible to accept the view that Jonah and the fish story are mere legend or even parable.

The book opens with the story of Jonah's commission from the Lord to go to the Assyrian capital of Nineveh and to preach against it, and Jonah's direct refusal to obey that command. Instead he boarded a ship going to Tarshish, in the opposite direction at the extreme west of the Mediterranean, to get as far away from Nineveh as possible. We are not told in the first chapter why Jonah did this, but the key to the book is in seeking the answer to the question: What made Jonah refuse to go to Nineveh?

Chapter 1 completes the story of Jonah's rebellious flight from his duty as a prophet. A great storm arose on the sea and the mariners became fearful that the ship was about to sink. When all their efforts seemed of no avail they cast lots to determine who was being punished by the gods through the instrument of this great storm. The lot fell upon Jonah who at that time was asleep in the inner part of the ship. Jonah confessed that he was fleeing from the presence of the Lord and, though the mariners tried to spare him, eventually they felt they had no choice but to cast him into the sea. Immediately upon doing this the storm quieted and the sailors were impressed by the power of Jonah's God and offered sacrifices to Him.

Jonah himself would have drowned but for the fact that a great fish, especially sent by the Lord, swallowed him and carried him in his belly for three days and three nights. Though popular reference almost always refers to the fish as a whale, there is no evidence that such was the case. The Hebrew uses the term fish rather than whale and in other places the word is translated sea monster.

Chapter 2 records the prayer Jonah uttered while in the belly of the fish. It is a compilation of various quotations from the Psalms and indicates both the general knowledge which Jonah had of the Scriptures and also the specific ones that came flashing into his mind as he found himself in the darkness amid the gastric juices of the great fish. The import of the verses he quotes is one of thanksgiving for his relationship to the living God, and a casting of himself upon God's mercy for deliverance. The chapter ends with the brief statement, "And the Lord spoke to the fish, and it vomited out Jonah upon the dry land" (2:10).

Once again the word of the Lord came to Jonah, commanding him to go to Nineveh and proclaim the message he had been sent to deliver. It is clear that God has changed the prophet's mind by his experience in the fish, but He has not changed His own mind one degree about what He wants Jonah to say to Nineveh. The description given of Nineveh is of "an exceedingly great city, three days' journey in breadth" (3:3). A day's journey was reckoned to be about 12 miles, so a three days' journey would be 36 miles. Nineveh was actually a group of cities, much like Los Angeles, clustered together on the banks of the Tigris River and forming the capital of the Assyrian empire.

The prophet went a day's journey into the city crying monotonously, "Yet forty days, and Nineveh shall be overthrown!" Ordinarily that kind of a message of destruction would not get much of a reception, for the Bible reports that other prophets were sent with messages of warning, but the people paid no attention. But an amazing thing happens. We are told that "the people of Nineveh believed God; they proclaimed a fast, and put on sackcloth, from the greatest of them to the least of them" (3:5). Even the king covered himself with sackcloth and sat in ashes, uttering a decree to urge the entire population to turn from their evil ways and violence with the hope that God would repent and save the city.

This is surely one of the most remarkable revivals ever recorded in history. That the city's repentance was genuine is indicated by the fact that God saw what they did and turned from the evil which He intended to bring against it, and the city was indeed spared. But another question remains unanswered. What potent factor caused the inhabitants of this great pagan city to repent so quickly and so thoroughly? This would be a continuing mystery were it not for a clue supplied by the Lord Jesus Christ Himself. In the Gospel of Luke, He refers to Jonah with these words: "For as Jonah became a sign to the men of Nineveh, so will the Son of man be to this generation" (Luke 11:30). He thus indicated that the prophet himself was the sign to the city which brought about their repentance. In the same manner He indicated He would be a sign to the whole generation of Israel and, beyond them, to the race of mankind.

What did He mean by this? There are Bible scholars who feel that something happened to Jonah in the fish's belly which changed his entire features. It seems highly likely that the prophet's skin was altered in appearance by the gastric juices of the fish. Dr. Harry Rimmer in his book *The Harmony of Science and Scripture* tells of an English sailor who fell overboard and was swallowed by a fish. A day or two later his shipmates saw the fish floating on the surface of the water. They caught it and took it ashore. When they opened it up, the sailors, to their amazement, found their shipmate alive. However, his skin had turned to chalky white and remained so for the rest of his life. Harry Rimmer personally talked with the man and learned from his own lips the details of his experience. There are probably in extant a half dozen accounts of individuals who have been swallowed by marine animals and survived.

It is not difficult to imagine what happened in the city of Nineveh when Jonah preached, if his entire face and body confirmed the remarkable story. The Ninevites would have clear proof that the God who sent Jonah to proclaim, "Yet forty days and Nineveh shall be overthrown," was a God who kept His word. Hence, the city repented to the last man and the judgment of God was stayed.

There have been some who have been troubled over the fact that Scripture says that God repented. This seems to indicate that He changed His mind from what He had previously determined to do. But this idea is difficult to square with the doctrine of God's omniscience and His sovereign determination of all events. We must remember, however, that these events are recorded for our information and instruction and therefore are written from a human point of view. God, of course, knew all the time that the city would repent at the preaching of Jonah under the peculiar circumstances in which he preached. And that also, from the apparent change in the divine actions, men would learn that repentance and contrition are the necessary conditions for a continuing relationship with the living God. Thus human repentance does not change God's mind, but actually carries forward His purpose. This whole story is an exemplification of the divine command, "Draw near to God and he will draw near to you" (Jas. 4:8). The city of Nineveh was spared and it was not until a hundred years later that God carried out His judgment on Nineveh and it was destroyed.

In the last chapter of the prophecy, we learn of the reaction of Jonah to God's mercy upon the pagan city. Here also we learn at last the reason why Jonah fled to Tarshish when the command first came to him to preach in Nineveh. The opening words of the chapter tell us that the prophet was angry when he saw the city was spared. In his anger he said: "I pray thee, Lord, is not this what I said when I was yet in my country? That is why I made haste to flee to Tarshish; for I knew that thou art a gracious God and merciful, slow to anger, and abounding in steadfast love, and repentest of evil" (Jonah 4:2).

It is clear from this that Jonah hated the Ninevites and would have liked nothing better than to see them destroyed. There was probably good reason for his hatred for the Ninevites were known throughout the entire world of that day as a cruel and ruthless people. Perhaps Jonah had actually seen several Ninevite invasions of Israel and the raiding and destruction of his people. He may have even suffered the loss of loved ones at the hands of these merciless soldiers, for the Ninevites had found more ingenious ways to be cruel than any other nation that had existed to that time. They were brutal, godless, and sinful, and for this reason the prophet wanted to see Nineveh destroyed.

One would have thought that he would have jumped at the chance to announce to this brutal city that they would meet their comeuppance in 40 days, but Jonah knew God better than that. In effect he says now to God, "I know you too well. If anyone by repenting gives you half a chance to be merciful, you'll change your mind and will not carry out your judgment against them." So to prevent that divine change of mind, Jonah fled to Tarshish.

What a revelation this gives of the character of God and the understanding of that character which these Old Testament prophets had. Critics today sometimes picture the God of the Old Testament as a vengeful, wrathful God, dealing only in black thunderclouds and lightning bolts, but that is not the kind of God Jonah knew. He knew that God was a gracious God, merciful and slow to anger, and abounding in love, quickly turning His judgments aside if there was any sign of repentant hearts.

The prophet was still in hopes that God would destroy the city; so he sat out on the rimrock looking over the city from the east and waited to see what God would do. Evidently he sat there for several days, for enough time elapsed for a gourd to grow and shade him from the hot sun. The prophecy informs us that it was God who appointed the gourd to thus bring relief to the prophet's discomfort. But the next day God also appointed a worm to destroy the plant and then sent a hot east wind to increase the heat and discomfort which Jonah felt.

Once again Jonah becomes angry at God and asks to have his life taken from him. But God responds with a beautiful word: "You pity the plant, for which you did not labor, nor did you make it grow, which came into being in a night, and perished in a night. And should not I pity Nineveh, that great city, in which there are more than a hundred and twenty thousand persons who do not know their right hand from their left, and also much cattle?" (4:10,11).

The reference to persons who do not know their right hand from their left is the Hebrew way of describing children. There were in Nineveh 120,000 little children as well as many animals, all of whom would be innocent victims of the sins of the adults under the avenging hand of God. Again, it is clear that God takes no delight in judgment, but seeks in long-suffering patience to bring individuals and even nations to the place of repentance and change.

The book ends rather abruptly at this point and we are not told whether Jonah learned his lesson or not. From the fact that he himself records this experience for us, it is most likely that he did learn. It is a lesson for all believers in all ages, that God loves the pagan world even if His people do not. How many of us would be delighted if tomorrow morning's paper reported that Moscow lay in smoking ruins? Yet we must never forget that God loves the Russians and the Chinese and any others who, at this present time, we call our national enemies.

Further, the lesson of this book is that God has sent us to the unbelieving peoples of the world as he sent Jonah to Nineveh. Around us also are the godless, the lawless, and the disobedient. We often dismiss them by saying, "How revolting! How disgusting! They deserve damnation." But God has sent us to be a sign to this generation. The sign is that of resurrection, as Jesus said it would be with Him. It is the sign of people who once were dead but have been made alive in Jesus Christ. The very skin of our faces should shine with a new brilliance which grace has brought to it, and thus we ought ourselves to be a sign of resurrected life to the hopeless and lost around us. But how like this stubborn prophet we often are, intent upon our own goals and our own comforts, and unconcerned about those who stumble in darkness around us.

MICAH

The prophet Micah came from the city of Moresheth, which is near Gath, about 30 miles from Jerusalem. He was a contemporary of Isaiah and his book is of a somewhat similar style. The prophet's name means "who is like God," and this forms the theme of his prophecy as well. Micah describes not only what God is like, but how man can be God-like.

The book divides easily into three parts. The first three chapters describe the failure of both Judah and Israel, and predict the judgment that would fall upon each. It is a vivid description of the lack of godliness in both nations. This is followed by a wonderful section in chapters 4 and 5, that describe the One who is coming, who is like God in every way. It is a great predictive section that looks forward to the coming of the Messiah. The last three chapters give us the pleading of God to the nation to lay hold of the secret of godliness.

Chapter 1, in striking language, describes the majestic approach of God striding forth in judgment upon His unrepentant people. Both the Assyrian and Babylonian invasions are in view in this passage, and the prophet describes in vivid and striking simile the fate of various cities as the invading forces come upon them. It is impossible to see this in English, but the Hebrew is a series of puns upon the names of the cities. For instance, Micah says, "Tell it not in Gath, weep not at all; in Beth-le-aphrah roll yourselves in the dust" (1:10). The name *Gath* means "weep" and the name *Beth-le-aphrah* means "dust town." Thus the passage would read something like this: "In Weep-town, weep not; in Dust-town, roll yourselves in the dust; in Beauty-town, beauty will be shamed; in Zaanan (which means "march") they will march not forth; in Neighbor-town they will end up with useless neighbors; and in Bitter-town they will grieve bitterly."

Chapter 2 goes on to picture vividly the destruction of the people, beginning with their rulers and reaching unto the women and the children. The prophet seems to be interrupted by false prophets who have protested his message, but to this objection Micah answers that God has changed His attitude toward the people because of their change toward Him. He speaks with great indignation against the false prophets who have misled the people.

In chapter 3 we are told the reason for the severity of judgment. Micah has been seeking godliness among the peoples of God and he looks where he might most expect to find it, among the rulers of the nation and the representatives of God. Instead, however, he finds corruption, oppression, bribery, and injustice. Thus Micah exposes the mess in Jerusalem and says that the reason God visits judgment is that those who have been given authority to act in God's stead have forgotten that they are responsible to God.

This touches us also, for whenever we find ourselves in a position of authority, we are told everywhere in Scripture to remember that we also have an Authority over us. The New Testament reminds us that masters are to remember they have a Master in heaven as well, and God holds all authority responsible to Him. The man who forgets this begins to use his power for his own advantage; and that is what had corrupted the nation in Micah's day and corrupts the peoples today. Micah sums this up for us in 3:11: "Its heads give judgment for a bribe, its priests teach for hire, its prophets divine for money; yet they lean upon the Lord and say, 'Is not the Lord in the midst of us? No evil shall come upon us.' " Here are mentioned all three classes of leaders in the nation—the spiritual rulers, the civil rulers, and the moral rulers. When such remember that they are representatives of God, there is always good government; but when they forget, there is corruption, oppression, bribery, agony and tears.

But in chapters 4 and 5, in a passage of wonderfully exalted vision, the prophet lifts up his eyes and looks across the centuries, past the rise of Assyria and Babylon, past the great eastern empire of Greece, past the Roman empire and the days of the Caesars, past the Middle Ages with Martin Luther and the Reformation, past the eighteenth century awakening under John Wesley, and even past our own day to the coming of One who is truly God-like. It is one of the most beautiful messianic passages in Scripture. The passage is almost identical with Isaiah 2:1-4. Since Isaiah and Micah were contemporaries, it is striking to note that they were both given the same vision of the glory that was ultimately to come to Israel. It begins with the exaltation of the Temple as a place of worship for all the nations of earth, and then narrows to a Person: "He shall judge between many peoples, and shall decide for strong nations afar off; and they shall beat their swords into plowshares, and their spears into pruning hooks; nation shall not lift up sword against nation, neither shall they learn war any more; but they shall sit every man under his vine and under his fig tree, and none shall make them afraid; for the mouth of the Lord of hosts has spoken" (Micah 4:3,4). Clearly that is a scene yet to come in world history. In the meantime, Joel's word must be fulfilled—that the nations beat their pruning hooks into spears and their plowshares into swords. They shall never forget how to make war and never obey this command of God until One comes who knows how to rule in godliness.

But Micah goes on to show that before that beautiful scene can be fulfilled, the nation must be carried away to Babylon, and then be restored at last to their land.

Chapter 5 opens with a new thought: "Now you are walled about with a wall; siege is laid against us; with a rod they strike upon the cheek the ruler of Israel." The historic fulfillment of this in the Gospels confirms that this is a picture of the Roman rule over Israel, when they would be contained like a city within a wall, and when the ruler of Israel would be struck on the cheek with a rod. When Jesus stood before Pilate, a crown of thorns was put upon His head and a robe of purple on Him, and the soldiers bowed before Him and mocked Him, striking Him on the cheek with their rods.

This application is confirmed by the next verse where the prophet sees where this mighty ruler is to come from. It is one of the great predictive passages of the Old Testament: "But you, O Bethlehem Ephrathah, who are little to be among the clans of Judah, from you shall come forth for me one who is to be ruler in Israel, whose origin is from of old, from ancient days" (5:2). When the wise men came from the East to Jerusalem they asked the chief priests, "Where is he that is born king of the Jews?" and the chief priests said that He would be found in Bethlehem. How did they know? It was because 700 years before, Micah had predicted that Bethlehem, though little among the cities of Judah, would be honored by being the birthplace of Him who was to be ruler of Israel.

The passage goes on to predict a time when Israel would wander in defeat, without a king, without a temple, without a sacrifice "until the time when she who is in travail has brought forth; then the rest of his brethren shall return to the people of Israel" (5:3). This indicates a gathering of Israel back to the land to join a nation which has already been partially restored.

Then the prophet sees the One who had come out of Bethlehem and describes Him thus: "And he shall stand and feed his flock in the strength of the Lord, in the majesty of the name of the Lord his God. And they shall dwell secure, for now he shall be great to the ends of the earth" (5:4). Looking thousands of years down the corridors of time, Micah clearly perceived One who would rise out of obscurity and fulfill all these predictions. He is the God-man, the only God-like man that ever walked on earth.

In the remaining verses of chapter 5 the prophet describes how this One shall cleanse the peoples of their iniquities and remove their idolatries from them, and execute His anger and wrath upon the nations that had oppressed them during the days of their exile from the land.

In chapters 6 and 7, in a passage of great power and beauty Jehovah pleads with His people to tell Him why they have turned from Him, and to give their reasons for their rejection of His loving ministry. Plaintively the Lord asks what He has done to them that they have rejected Him so, and in what way He has wearied them. In answer, the people sarcastically say: "With what shall I come before the Lord, and bow myself before God on High? Shall I come before him with burnt offerings, with calves a year old? Will the Lord be pleased with thousands of rams, with ten thousands of rivers of oil? Shall I give my first-born for my transgression, the fruit of my body for the sin of my soul?" (6:6,7). The people are asking, "What more can we do that we have not done? We have brought the required offerings, and still God is not satisfied. What more can we bring? Shall we even do like the pagans around and offer our children? Will that please God?"

To this blasphemous response, the prophet declares: "He has showed you, O man, what is good; and what does the Lord require of you but to do justice, and to love kindness, and to walk humbly with your God?" (6:8). This is perhaps the most oft-quoted verse from the prophecy of Micah, and is the favorite of many who feel that God's only requirement for salvation is a virtuous life. But that is to ignore the fact that to walk humbly before one's God involves a full acceptance of God's provision for personal redemption and salvation through the sacrifice of Another on our behalf. The way to God-likeness is to put away our wickedness by confessing our guilt before God, and looking to Him to pardon our iniquities and to cast our sins into the depths of the sea.

Because Israel refused to do this, the prophet goes on in the remainder of chapter 6 and the early part of chapter 7 to resume the theme of judgment, but concludes his message with a marvelous picture of the mercy of God. Notice especially the question with which he begins: "Who is a God like thee, pardoning iniquity and passing over transgression for the remnant of his inheritance? He does not retain his anger forever because he delights in steadfast love. He will again have compassion upon us, he will tread our iniquities under foot. Thou wilt cast all our sins into the depths of the sea. Thou wilt show faithfulness to Jacob and steadfast love to Abraham, as thou hast sworn to our fathers from the days of old" (7:18-20).

From the New Testament we learn that the way to walk humbly before our God is to walk in the light as He is in the light, that is, to walk openly and in honesty. Do not try to hide anything from God. Do not pretend to be something you are not in His presence. Walk in the light as He is in the light and as John assures us: "The blood of Jesus His Son cleanses us from all sin" (1 John 1:7). So Micah's question rings in our ears—Who is like God? Well, the only answer is, the God-like person is the one who walks with Jesus Christ—God Himself become man—who imparts to us His own likeness.

CHAPTER ELEVEN

God Answers

NAHUM

The two prophets, Nahum and Habakkuk, both deal with a common problem in the life of believers: the anger we often feel at God when He does not act as we expect Him to.

Nahum's name means "comfort" and though the prophet's message is conveyed in strong and forceful language, nevertheless his message is basically one of comfort to the southern kingdom of Judah. He prophesied at the height of Assyrian power after Sennacherib had invaded the kingdom and the northern kingdom of Israel had been carried away into Assyrian exile. It looked as though Judah would shortly suffer the same fate, but Nahum was sent to declare that it was rather the seemingly resistless might of Assyria that would be crushed and judged. There was warning in this too for Judah; but the essential message of Nahum was that God answers the plight of His people and moves in unexpected ways to deliver them.

Very little is known of the prophet Nahum except that he came from the village of Elkosh, whose location is uncertain. There is some indication that it was in Galilee and it is interesting to note that the name Capernaum on

the Sea of Galilee literally means "the village of Nahum."
The prophet's message is directed against Nineveh, the
same Nineveh we saw humbled and repenting under Jonah's ministry. But Nahum prophesied some 70 years
after Jonah's day and by his time the Assyrian capital had
fallen again into its violent and degraded ways.

The prophecy opens with a striking vision of the
majesty and might of God. He is described as a God of
zealous consistency in defending His holy and righteous
character. Yet He is slow to anger and, though merciful,
is never mocked. The prophet sees Him as moved at last
by the wickedness and cruelty of the Assyrians to permit
His anger to burn in terrible fury. We can get some idea of
the awfulness of the divine anger in the fact that every
Hebrew word for anger is compacted together in the first
nine verses. They combine to picture God as burning with
a terrible blistering rage.

Yet He does not strike out in all directions, as in a
temper tantrum, but directs His rage against those who are
most guilty. Verses 11 through 15 most probably describe
the Assyrian king Sennacherib who had invaded Judah in
the days of Hezekiah, as recorded in Isaiah 36 and 37. He
is described by Nahum as one who came "out from you,
who plotted evil against the Lord, and counseled villainy"
(1:11). But in verse 14 the prophet says: "The Lord has
given commandment about you: 'No more shall your
name be perpetuated; from the house of your gods I will
cut off the graven image and the molten image. I will
make your grave, for you are vile' " (1:14). This was
fulfilled literally in the murder of Sennacherib who, while
worshiping in the temple of his gods, was struck down
and murdered by his sons who then took his throne.

Verse 15 seems to reflect the joyful shout that went up
from Jerusalem when news was brought of Sennacherib's
death. "Behold, on the mountains the feet of him who
brings good tidings, who proclaims peace! Keep your

feasts, O Judah, fulfill your vows, for never again shall the wicked come against you, he is utterly cut off" (1:15).

In chapter 2 the prophet looks on to describe in vivid detail the siege and fall of Nineveh, which historically occurred in 612 B.C. when the Babylonians and Medes finally overthrew the city. The entire chapter is a remarkable dirge which vividly describes the attacking army, the red uniforms of the Babylonians, the raging of their chariots through the streets of the city, and the drunken, half-asleep responses of the Assyrians as they stumbled to their assigned defense posts.

Verse 6 says, "The river gates are opened, the palace is in dismay." The historian Diodurus Siculus, writing in the first century B.C., declares: "There was an old prophecy that Nineveh should not be taken until the river became an enemy to the city. And in the third year of the seige, the river being swollen with continual rains, overflowed every part of the city and broke down the wall for twenty furlongs. Then the king, thinking that the oracle was fulfilled and the river become an enemy to the city, built a large funeral pile in the palace and, collecting together all his wealth and his concubines and eunuchs, burned himself and the palace with them all, and the enemy entered at the breach that the waters had made and took the city." Thus Nahum's prophecy was fulfilled in precise detail.

In the latter part of chapter 2 the prophet predicts that Nineveh's destruction would bring about total desolation, and this was fulfilled so completely that when Alexander the Great marched across the site of Nineveh in 331 B.C., he did not know that a great city had once stood there. It was not until 1845 that the site of Nineveh was identified and its ruins uncovered.

Chapter 3 states the reasons for the overthrow of Nineveh. The prophet declares, "Woe to the bloody city, all full of lies and booty—no end to the plunder!" (3:1). God's anger is awakened because of the legendary cruelty

of the Assyrian armies and their ruthless plundering of the
nations around by means of deceptive agreements which
they broke without warning or regard.

In verse 8 the prophet asks, "Are you better than
Thebes that sat by the Nile, with water around her, her
rampart a sea, and water her wall?" This great city of
Egypt was located some 400 miles up the Nile and was
regarded as one of the impregnable fortresses of the day,
yet it was destroyed by Ashurbanipal in 663 B.C. God thus
warns Nineveh that if such a great city could fall, so
Nineveh's overthrow was equally possible. The prophecy
ends with the words, "There is no assuaging your hurt,
your wound is grievous. All who hear the news of you
clap their hands over you. For upon whom has not come
your unceasing evil?" (3:19). The Assyrians attempted to
gain rule over all of western Asia and were universally
despised. When Nineveh was destroyed there was rejoicing throughout the whole of the known world for Assyrian
arrogance and cruelty was hated everywhere.

Thus Nahum's word brought comfort to a nation
threatened by a godless, cruel and rapacious foe. Yet
Scripture speaks of a latter-day Assyrian which shall rise
as a godless and cruel power, which again will dominate
the world of the end times. It is not surprising that many
Bible scholars have identified this with Russia. It is striking that here the Lord addresses Nineveh twice saying,
"Behold, I am against you"; and in Ezekiel's description
of the invasion of Israel by the northern army in the last
days, he begins chapter 39 with similar words, "Behold, I
am against you, O Gog, chief prince of Meshech and
Tubal." Perhaps it is time again to reassert God's capacity
for anger and judgment. It is a mistake to think that God is
so loving that He cannot punish sin, for as Charles Spur-
geon has said, "He who does not believe that God will
punish sin will not believe that He will pardon it through
the blood of His Son."

HABAKKUK

The little prophecy of Habakkuk is undoubtedly one of the most important books in all the Bible, for it answers the question, "Why does God permit the righteous to suffer and the wicked to flourish?"

Habakkuk was a contemporary of Jeremiah who ministered in Judah, as Jeremiah did, just before the Babylonian invasion. It was a time of gross spiritual decline and widespread injustice within the nation. The name *Habakkuk* means "the embracer." It suggests the picture of a father whose son has been injured by some passing bully and he gathers up the hurt child and comforts him while bitterness enters his own heart. He cries out in perplexity, "Why doesn't God do something? How can a just God permit such wrong?"

So the prophet Habakkuk gathered up the hurt of Judah and the righteous remnant within it and cried out in perplexity at the seeming silence of God. His first cry is: "Why dost thou make me see wrongs and look upon trouble? Destruction and violence are before me; strife and contention arise. So the law is slacked and justice never goes forth" (1:3,4).

God answers in verses 5 through 11, saying in effect, "I am doing something. I am raising up the Chaldeans to punish the wicked in Israel. I am not indifferent, but am moving to judge evil."

But this brings no relief to the troubled prophet, for if he was puzzled by the apparent inactivity of God against the wickedness of the rulers of Israel, he is now even more troubled by the problem of how a righteous and holy God can use an ungodly nation to punish His own people. The Chaldeans are well known for their crass indifference to human suffering, and their gross immorality and callous luxury. So the prophet asks, "Is he then to keep on emptying his net, and mercilessly slaying nations forever?" (1:17).

When no answer comes to his tormented question, the prophet retreats to his watchtower where in silence he will wait for God's reply. Soon the answer comes for the Lord commands him to write that a day of judgment awaits the Chaldeans as well, but it will not be immediately. Habakkuk is encouraged by the words, "If it seem slow, wait for it; it will surely come, it will not delay" (2:3). And then he is given the key message of the entire Bible, "Behold, he whose soul is not upright in him shall fail, but the righteous shall live by his faith" (2:4). This verse is quoted three times in the New Testament—in Romans, Galatians, and Hebrews. In each of these great books a different emphasis is underscored. In Romans the emphasis is upon the words "the righteous." In Galatians, it is upon the words "shall live." While in Hebrews the emphasis is upon the words "by his faith." Literally the verse declares that the unrighteous soul is puffed up and is thus "not upright in him." It is a picture of pride and its effect upon the human ego. It puffs it up in arrogance and self-sufficiency. As a result, the unrighteous perish, but the man or woman of faith is living by another principle. It is a confidence that God is at work and will not fail to fulfill His determined purposes. The result of that is life. Faith then is the principle of life, in spite of all appearances at the present moment; but pride is the principle of death, despite the present appearances.

The prophet is then shown five woes which are addressed against the characteristics of pride. The first, ambition, is denounced. The ambitious man carries within himself the seed of his own destruction, for he is ultimately crushed by the ambitions of others. The greedy likewise overreach themselves and lose all. The violent man ends by destroying himself. The insolent man becomes sated with his contempt, and thus the cup of judgment in the Lord's right hand comes 'round to him as well. The idolator trusts his own creation and finds himself left without help in the day of his own need. So Habakkuk is reassured that the Chaldean onslaught against Judah will not be left unavenged, for the attacker carries the seed of his own destruction within himself. The prophet is left with the words, "But the Lord is in his holy temple; let all the earth keep silence before him" (2:20).

In the third chapter Habakkuk is granted a vision of God moving in judgment against the proud. It comes as an answer to his prayer in which he requests that God will make known to him both His wrath and His mercy. In majestic and moving poetry, the prophet then reveals the might and glory of God which he saw. "His brightness was like the light, rays flashed from his hand; and there he veiled his power. Before him went pestilence, and plague followed close behind. He stood and measured the earth; he looked and shook the nations; then the eternal mountains were scattered, the everlasting hills sank low. His ways were as of old" (3:4-6). He goes on to describe God as striding the earth in fury, trampling the nations in His anger, as crushing the head of the wicked and stripping him naked before the world.

As a result of such a vision, the prophet declares, "I hear, and my body trembles, my lips quiver at the sound; rottenness enters into my bones, my steps totter beneath me. I will quietly wait for the day of trouble to come upon people who invade us" (3:16). Thus he has learned that when God gives a promise, those who wait in faith will surely see its fulfillment. Meanwhile, their faith is the principle of life for them despite the circumstances.

And so his puzzled cry turns at last to singing and the prophet closes the prophecy with these beautiful words: "Though the fig tree do not blossom, nor fruit be on the vines, the produce of the olive fail and the fields yield no food, the flock be cut off from the fold and there be no herd in the stalls, yet I will rejoice in the Lord, I will joy in the God of my salvation. God, the Lord, is my strength; he makes my feet like hinds' feet, he makes me tread upon my high places" (3:17-19).

The application of this to our own hearts is plain. We, too, live in the days of the apparent silence of God. Under a silent heaven, we watch injustice and cruelty and violence rule the earth. Nothing seems to intervene, and our heart questions, "Is God too weak or too indifferent to help us?" But the answer is that evil and injustice has already received its death blow. On a cross outside Jerusalem God has done all He needs to do to end the blight of sin, except for the actual destruction of the wicked. His last word spoken to the race was that of love and grace uttered on the cross. His next word must be wrath and judgment, but as Peter tells us, He is long-suffering, "not wishing that any should perish" (2 Pet. 3:9). The word of Habakkuk is that faith waits in confidence that God will complete His work in His own good time, and meantime we, like the prophet, may rejoice in the fact that the Lord is our strength. As Psalm 50:3 puts it: "Our God comes, he does not keep silence."

CHAPTER TWELVE

God Is Jealous

ZEPHANIAH

In the fourth chapter of the Gospel of Luke, we are told of an occasion when Jesus went into the synagogue at Nazareth, His hometown. There was given to Him the book of the prophecy of Isaiah to read. Opening the scroll He found the place where it read, "The Spirit of the Lord is upon me, because he has anointed me to preach good news to the poor" (Luke 4:18). The passage goes on to describe the ministry of the Messiah, and Jesus read it until He reached the sentence, "To proclaim the acceptable year of the Lord" (v. 19). At this point Jesus stopped His reading and handed the scroll back to the attendant saying, "Today this scripture has been fulfilled in your hearing" (v. 21). The remarkable thing about this incident is that Jesus stopped His reading in the middle of a sentence, for Isaiah goes on to say "and the day of vengeance of our God" (Isa. 61:2). Jesus did not read that last sentence because it was not yet time to proclaim the day of vengeance of God. That day of vengeance is coming and Jesus said much more about it in His great Olivet Discourse, but it was yet many centuries in the future from when Jesus read the verse in the synagogue.

It is this "day of vengeance" which is the theme of the

prophecy of Zephaniah. The prophet's name means "hidden of the Lord" and he speaks as though he were a representative of the remnant of faith, those few people who remain true to God during the time of great trouble that is to come upon the earth. They will be hidden by God Himself and watched over by divine love to keep them during this time. It is of these people that the book of Zephaniah is written, and especially of the great day of the Lord which is vividly described in this prophecy.

The prophet identifies himself as a great, great grandson of Hezekiah, one of the great and godly kings of Judah. His ministry occurred during the days of Josiah, the last godly king of Judah. Perhaps the ministry of Zephaniah had much to do with the reforms which Josiah instituted during his reign. Since Josiah was also a descendant of Hezekiah, it meant that he and the prophet Zephaniah were related members of the royal family. Zephaniah begins his prophecy with a vivid description of the coming judgment under Nebuchadnezzar, though he describes it as "the day of the Lord." The detail of destruction which he envisions was clearly fulfilled by the Babylonian invasion.

We must recognize there is a great deal of difference between the day of the Lord and the Lord's day. Sunday is the Lord's day, for it was the day when our Lord arose from the dead. But the day of the Lord is the day of the manifestation of God's hand directly in human affairs. At the present hour even though God is working through the events of history bringing about overthrows, uprisings, and calamities as well as periods of prosperity and blessing, nevertheless His hand is hidden in the glove of history. But all the writers of Scripture agree that a day is coming when God will intervene directly in the affairs of men again. Notice how Zephaniah uses the personal pronoun throughout this passage: "*I* will utterly sweep away everything from the face of the earth, says the Lord."

Again, "*I* will sweep away man and beast," etc.

Beginning with verse 14, as in many of the prophecies, the prophet's vision lifts to encompass another day far down the corridors of time which will be the last great judgment of God upon earth. He calls it "the great day of the Lord" and describes it thus: "A day of wrath is that day, a day of distress and anguish, a day of ruin and devastation, a day of darkness and gloom, a day of clouds and thick darkness, a day of trumpet blast and battle cry against the fortified cities and against the lofty battlements" (1:15,16). This describes a time of such great and universal trouble that there will be nothing comparable to it in all the annals of history.

Zephaniah goes on to say, "I will bring distress on men, so that they shall walk like the blind, because they have sinned against the Lord; their blood shall be poured out like dust, and their flesh like dung. Neither their silver nor their gold shall be able to deliver them on the day of the wrath of the Lord" (1:17,18). We must always remember in reading passages like this that it is not easy for God to speak this way. He Himself declares that He takes no delight in the death of the wicked. Judgment, one prophet says, is His strange work, for His heart delights in mercy. But eventually, if His will is to be done, and if earth at last is to attain to the glorious freedom described in the prophets concerning mankind, if the dreams that lie hidden away in the hearts of men for a warless world and a great time of prosperity when joy will flood the earth—if that is ever to come, then God must deal with the entrenched evil of men. This is why the coming of a day of vengeance is absolutely certain. All the prophets warn of this and the New Testament writers refer frequently to it as well.

In Zephaniah's second chapter, he traces the extent of God's destruction. Certain nations are named outright. The ancient enemy of Israel, Philistia, will be made desolate. Moab and Ammon will be destroyed and their land become like Sodom and Gomorrah. The Ethiopians will be slain and the great nation of Assyria will be judged, with its capital, Nineveh, rendered a desolation and a dry waste in the desert.

Finally in chapter 3 the judgment centers upon the city of Jerusalem. Its case is hopeless from the human standpoint. Its evil is so widespread and so deeply imbedded that there is no likelihood of correction from within. All her leaders are corrupted and faithless so that the nation lies hopeless and helpless, awaiting its deserved judgment.

But in the midst of this, there comes a gleam of hope: " 'Therefore, wait for me,' says the Lord, 'for the day when I arise as a witness. For my decision is to gather nations to assemble kingdoms, to pour out upon them my indignation, all the heat of my anger; for in the fire of my jealous wrath all the earth shall be consumed' " (3:8).

In the midst of this universal judgment, Jehovah promises to bring relief to the suffering of Judah, and He declares: "For I will leave in the midst of you a people humble and lowly. They shall seek refuge in the name of the Lord, those who are left in Israel; they shall do no wrong and utter no lies, nor shall there be found in their mouth a deceitful tongue. For they shall pasture and lie down, and none shall make them afraid" (3:12,13). Thus even in the midst of His judgments, God would preserve Himself a people who would remain faithful to His cause. In beautiful language, the prophet depicts the character of those who will be redeemed. They shall be "humble and lowly" for they have been conquered by the sovereign grace of God.

The closing verses, from 14 on, constitute a command to the redeemed in Zion to break into praise to the Lord in song for the redemption He has brought about. This is the new order that follows the darkness, the gloom, and the slaughter. It is what God has been aiming at all along, that He might bring song instead of sorrow, service instead of selfishness, security instead of slavery. The prophet's picture is one of great beauty and glory. He describes the scene thus: "The Lord, your God, is in your midst, a warrior who gives victory; he will rejoice over you with gladness, he will renew you in his love; he will exult over you with loud singing as on a day of festival" (3:17). It is the song of the redeemed in which the Lord Himself is present to lead them in glorious exultation.

All this is possible to believers at the level of the spirit right now. When God deals a death stroke against the flesh within us and brings us through the painful judgment of saying no to the ego and the self life, there follows a time of singing and of joy. That is the reason God takes us through the pain and the darkness. What we see to be true of the individual life today will ultimately be true on the whole wide canvas of history as God brings the evil of humanity to an end and ushers in the day of joy and gladness.

HAGGAI

Earlier in this volume we noted the fact that the Old Testament is naturally divided into two major sections, each one covering in general the same period of time. The Old Testament begins with Genesis and the account of the patriarchs Abraham, Isaac, Jacob, and Joseph, but then narrows its vision to trace the family of Abraham through Moses and the Exodus with its new beginning, with entrance into the land of Canaan. The history of Israel in the land is followed through the period of the Judges, the beginning of the monarchy under, first, Saul and then David, and finally the story is traced through the succession of kings of both Israel and Judah to the final exile of Israel to Assyria and Judah to Babylon. The books of Ezra, Nehemiah, and Esther, which close the first half of the Old Testament, give us glimpses of life in Babylon and record the return from Babylon to Jerusalem and the beginnings of the worship of Jehovah again in a Temple in Jerusalem.

This second half of the Old Testament begins again with the period of the patriarchs, going back to the story of Job and his struggles to learn what God wanted him to know about God and himself. Through the books of Psalms, Proverbs, and Song of Solomon the inner life of the people of God is traced during the period roughly from Moses to David and Solomon. Then the prophets brought before us the struggles of the people of God during increasing declension and spiritual idolatry until at last the period of exile is reached.

Now once again we have come to the time of restoration from Babylon, and the ministry of the three postexilic prophets, Haggai, Zechariah, and Malachi. These three prophets ministered in Judah after the return from the Babylonian captivity as recounted in the book of Ezra when the people began to lay the foundations of the Temple. However, because of political and local problems, the work ceased and Haggai begins his ministry with one theme in view: "Let us arise and build the house of the Lord."

Because of this continuing emphasis the prophecy of Haggai has been a favorite book for all preachers today who are trying to get their congregations to build adequate buildings. But it is a misuse and misunderstanding of Scripture to apply it in that way. In Haggai's day, the Lord's house was the Temple. Although the returned people were still under the domain and rule of the Babylonians, they had permission from the king of Babylon to begin work on the Temple. Haggai delivers four messages to the people, all uttered within the space of a year and a half, and all concerning the need to build the Temple. But this becomes for us a picture of our responsibility as believers today to build the true house of God, which is not a building, but people. Each believer is the Temple of God and collectively all believers form the great house of God which is the church, the place where God dwells. The proper application of the prophecy of Haggai to our own time is therefore to see it as an exhortation to the people of God everywhere concerning their responsibility to make the worship of God and the holiness of the church of God their first concern.

Haggai's four messages are carefully dated. The first one includes all of chapter 1. It was addressed to the civil governor, Zerubbabel, and to the religious head, Joshua, the chief priest. Each message reveals an excuse given by the people for not working on the Temple, and what God saw to be the real reason behind that excuse. So to the leaders of the people Haggai says, "Thus says the Lord of hosts: This people say the time has not yet come to rebuild the house of the Lord" (Haggai 1:2).

After the laying of the foundation, the work of building the Temple had been abandoned for 15 years. The reason the people gave was that some mistake had been made in figuring the 70 years that Jeremiah prophesied. They were suggesting there was no use doing anything because God was not yet ready to move. But God answered their excuse in these words, "Then the word of the Lord came by Haggai the prophet, 'Is it a time for you yourselves to dwell in your paneled houses, while this house lies in ruins? Now therefore thus says the Lord of hosts: Consider how you have fared' " (1:4,5). Ironically, God suggests that the real reason the work of building has lagged is that they are all wrapped up in their own affairs. They did not feel it was time to build God's house, but they had no doubt that it was time for God to help them build theirs! Clearly they had forgotten that the fact they were in the land at all proves that God's time had come. They would not have been back in Palestine had the 70 years not been fulfilled. The real reason for their indolence was that they were not willing to put God's concerns first.

So the prophet invites them to consider what the results have been in their lives. Twice he uses the phrase "Consider how you have fared" (vv. 5,9). Their harvests were poor, their clothing inadequate, their returns could not keep pace with inflation. Furthermore, they were neglecting the Temple while adequate supplies of wood were available on the hillsides of Israel to build the house of the Lord. So the Lord reminds them, "Therefore the heavens above you have withheld the dew, and the earth has withheld its produce. And I have called for a drought upon the land and the hills, upon the grain, the new wine, the oil, upon what the ground brings forth, upon men and cattle, and upon all their labors" (1:10,11).

Why did God do this? Was He trying to punish them? No, God does not punish in that sense. He was trying to wake them up. He was attempting to recall them to a reappraisal of their priorities and a remembrance of a rule which runs through all of Scripture and through life, "Seek first his kingdom and his righteousness, and all these things shall be yours as well" (Matt. 6:33).

The result of this forceful reminder was that the people began work immediately upon the Temple, and Haggai was sent to encourage them with the word of the Lord, "I am with you, says the Lord" (Hag. 1:13).

How long did the work last? Three weeks; then it ground to a halt again. Twenty-one days after his first message, the word of the Lord came to Haggai once more. "Speak now to Zerubbabel the son of She-alti-el, governor of Judah, and to Joshua the son of Jehozadak, the high priest, and to all the remnant of the people, and say, 'Who is left among you that saw this house in its former glory? How do you see it now? Is it not in your sight as nothing?' " (2:2,3).

A comparison of this passage with Ezra 3 indicates that Jehovah was simply repeating here what the people had been using as a further excuse to stop work on the Temple. Certain old men had come down to watch the work who had been but children when they were carried captive into Babylon. They had seen the Temple of Solomon in all its glory and, as old men sometimes do, they were living in the past. They said to the people, "Do you call this a Temple, this heap of ruins here? We saw Solomon's Temple and what you are building is nothing compared to that. We remember the gold and silver that was in his Temple and you do not have any gold or silver. How are you going to decorate this Temple?" The people grew discouraged at this and said in effect, "You know, they're right. We don't have any gold or silver; we don't have anything to make this Temple beautiful. What's the use? Why work?" So they quit.

Once again the word of the Lord was, "Work, for I am with you, says the Lord of hosts, according to the promise I made you when you came out of Egypt. My Spirit abides among you; fear not" (2:4,5). Jehovah goes on to promise He would shake the political powers of the day so that they would pour gold and silver into the land. But even more significantly He says, "The latter splendor of this house shall be greater than the former, says the Lord of hosts; and in this place I will give prosperity, says the Lord of hosts" (v. 9).

These words were fulfilled after 400 years when the same Temple, changed and altered by Herod the Great but the same essential building, was entered by Jesus of Nazareth and was filled with the glory of His teaching, standing in the midst of the Temple and saying things that the people had never heard before. By those words He utterly changed the life of that nation and every nation in the world since. Thus the glory of the second Temple was a greater and different glory than that of Solomon's.

But the people quit work again and two months later a third message was given to the prophet Haggai: "Thus says the Lord of hosts: Ask the priests to decide this question, 'If one carries holy flesh in the skirt of his garment, and touches with his skirt bread, or pottage, or wine, or oil, or any kind of food, does it become holy?' " (2:11,12). To this question the priests properly answered no. The prophet then pointed out that any person who is unclean contaminates everything he touches, and by this the people were to learn that the ruined and neglected Temple had been the cause for all the economic difficulties which they had experienced for so long. But now that they had begun to build, the prophet reassured them that divine blessing would not be far behind.

The final word of Haggai is a personal message to Zerubbabel, the governor. It is a reminder that the Lord is in charge of all the nations of the earth, and promises to shake the kingdoms of earth so that continual instability will mark the days of Zerubbabel's governorship, but he himself is given reassurance: "On that day, says the Lord of hosts, I will take you, O Zerubbabel my servant, the son of She-alti-el, says the Lord, and make you like a signet ring; for I have chosen you, says the Lord of hosts" (2:23). This was undoubtedly a great personal encouragement to the governor, but it clearly views him also as typifying the messianic King who, as the chosen of God, would bear the signet ring of authority upon His hand and would build a Temple not made with hands, which would remain when all earthly kingdoms and governments are shaken and destroyed.

CHAPTER THIRTEEN

God Encourages

ZECHARIAH

The prophet Zechariah was a young contemporary of Haggai. Both ministered to the remnant of the people who had returned from captivity in Babylon. It was a discouraging and depressing time for, although they were back in Jerusalem and the rebuilding of the Temple had begun, they were still vassals of Babylon, subject to the Gentile powers around them, without much hope for the future.

The dating of God's first message to Zechariah indicates that it fell between two of the messages which Haggai had addressed to the people. Thus both of these prophets were attempting to awaken the people to new hope and new activity.

Zechariah introduces himself as the son of Berechiah, who was in turn the son of Iddo, the prophet. These names are significant, for *Zechariah* means "God remembers," *Berechiah* means "God blesses" and *Iddo* means "at the appointed time." Thus even in the prophets' names God has hidden the theme of the book of Zechariah, for His message was a reminder that God remembered His people and would bless them at the appointed time.

The prophecy of Zechariah has been called "The Apocalypse of the Old Testament," for like the book of

Revelation, it is an unveiling of the unseen things. That is what *apocalypse* means, a revelation, an unveiling. However, in Zechariah Israel is in the foreground and the Gentile nations in the background, while in the book of Revelation the reverse is true.

Zechariah 1:2,3 gives a brief summary of the book in outline form. It reads: "The Lord was very angry with your fathers. Therefore say to them Thus says the Lord of hosts: Return to me, says the Lord of hosts, and I will return to you, says the Lord of hosts."

Three divisions of Zechariah's prophecy are indicated by the repetition of the dramatic name "the Lord of hosts." This is one of the unusual names of God in the Scriptures, and means "God of the masses," the Lord of *all* hosts—whether angel, human, demonic, whatever. Even the stars are referred to in Scripture as the hosts, and whatever hosts or masses may be in view. Jehovah is the God who is sovereign over them all.

The statement that indicates the first division is: "The Lord was very angry with your fathers." This is then enlarged upon in verses 4-6, describing God's displeasure with His people.

The theme of the second division is described by the words, "Return to me," and from 1:7 to 6:15 Zechariah tells of God's program to deliver His people and bring them back to Himself.

The third division, chapters 7-14, is an exposition of the words in verse 3 of chapter 1, "And I will return to you, says the Lord of hosts." This is always the program of God. If anyone finds himself straying away from the Divine Presence so that life grows cold and faith grows dim, exposing him to great temptations and pressures toward evil, the only recourse is to turn to the Lord. If you want God back in your life with all the glory His presence entails, then come back to Him. That is the formula for recovery.

The first division is a brief reminder by the prophet that the history of Israel has been one of departing from the words and ways of God. There is no need for the prophet to enlarge on this, for the long years of captivity in Babylon were sufficient confirmation that moral departure brings God's displeasure.

The Second Division

Beginning with 1:7, a most remarkable vision was given to the prophet. It was actually eight visions in one which were all shown to Zechariah on the same night. These eight visions fall into three major divisions which may be likened to three acts in a great drama revealed to the prophet. As we read them we may imagine ourselves as spectators to this drama which God is unfolding to Zechariah. God is the Author; Zechariah is the producer; and we are the audience.

The entire vision covers the time from Zechariah's day through all of subsequent history to the return of the Lord to His people in power and glory. The first act is made up of two visions. The prophet sees a Watcher looking out over the people in a valley. The Watcher is riding upon a horse, and with him are other riders upon horses. The angel of the Lord interprets the vision to the prophet. It means simply that Israel—symbolized here by the lowly myrtle shrub—were the people shadowed in the valley, watched over by a divine Watcher. The returned exiles could clearly see that they were indeed in a shadowed place, but what they could not see was the One who was watching the whole procedure, who had with Him great resources to meet their need in the hour of despair. This was what the vision revealed to them.

The second vision in the first act reveals four smiths or workmen—actually carpenters. The prophet saw four horns and four carpenters, and this too is interpreted to the prophet. Like the riders in the first vision, the four carpen-

ters are divine agents who are sent out to terrify the
nations, symbolized by the four horns. The people of
Zechariah's day were discouraged by the seeming invinci-
bility of the great powers arrayed against them, but what
they did not see was the divine resources. They were
unconscious of the divine agents who were there to move
on their behalf, and that is what God revealed to them.

Thus the curtain falls at the end of Act one, and in the
second chapter it rises on Act two, which is but a single
vision. It was the vision of a man with a measuring line in
his hand who went out to measure the city of Jerusalem;
and as he did this the interpreting angel said to the prophet: "Jerusalem shall be inhabited as villages without
walls, because of the multitude of men and cattle in it. For
I will be to her a wall of fire round about, says the Lord
and I will be the glory within her" (2:4,5).

This is followed by a beautiful description of the days
of blessing which are to come upon Israel, all to be
literally fulfilled as Israel would be brought into the place
of blessing in the land. It was God's way of saying to the
people, "Come back to me and blessing will flow to you."
Blessing can come from no other source. It is only from
the resources of God that joy, love and peace can flow.
The man with the measuring line was sent to highlight, by
contrast, the measureless blessings God was ready to pour
out to those who returned to a relationship with Him.

Act three consists of five more visions. Here the way
to return to God is acted out in five steps. In the first scene
Joshua the high priest is revealed, standing before God.
Opposed to him is Satan, the adversary. The people of
Zechariah's day knew well that Satan was against them,
but what they could not see was the Advocate, the One
who stood on their behalf and ministered for them. Then,
in this wonderfully moving vision, the prophet saw how
Joshua was cleansed. His filthy garments were taken off
and he was clad in new, clean garments. The reason for

this was given: "I have chosen Jerusalem" (see 3:2). The way this cleansing of God's chosen people would occur is then clearly described: "Hear now, O Joshua the high priest, you and your friends who sit before you, for they are men of good omen: behold, I will bring my servant the Branch. For behold, upon the stone which I have set before Joshua, upon a single stone with seven facets, I will engrave its inscription, says the Lord of hosts, and I will remove the guilt of this land in a single day" (3:8,9).

This is a marvelous prophecy of the coming of Jehovah's servant, the Branch. He would be a great stone upon which God would make certain engravings (this, perhaps, refers to the marks of crucifixion), and by Him the guilt of the land would be removed in a single day. It is clear in this vision that cleansing is the first step in the way back.

Then in Scene two we learn what follows the cleansing of God. It is a vision of a lampstand and two olive trees. The trees continually dripped oil from their branches into the lampstand, which was burning brightly. Oil is everywhere in Scripture used symbolically of the Holy Spirit, and this is a wonderfully symbolic description of the truth that God will dwell within, supplying inner resource that makes it possible for His own to burn brightly as lights in the midst of a dark generation. Thus the word of the Lord was addressed particularly to Zerubbabel, the governor, saying: "This is the word of the Lord to Zerubbabel: Not by might nor by power, but by my Spirit, says the Lord of hosts" (4:6).

Scene three (5:1-4) describes a flying scroll with writing on both sides, containing curses against thieves and those who blaspheme among the people. It was a picture of the law in the midst of corruption. The people could see the corruption in their midst, but they could not see the law, so this is God's encouragement in the hour of darkness, that God's law was still at work, bringing a curse upon lawlessness, bringing it ultimately to an end.

In Scene four (5:5-11), Zechariah saw a woman in an ephah, which was a measure of grain very much like our bushel basket. While the prophet and the interpreting angel watched, wings were given to this basket and it flew away to Babylon. Though the prophet is given no explanation of this, it is possible to interpret it because it contains terms which are used elsewhere in Scripture. Whenever a woman appears as symbolic of evil it is always a reference to something religiously wrong. Here then is the picture of the judgment of false faith, very much as in the book of Revelation, where a woman who is the false church is called "mystery: 'Babylon the great' " (Rev. 17:5). Zechariah sees God's judgment falling upon hypocritical religions. The people could see the hypocrisy of their religious leaders, but they could not see the power of God to identify it as Babylonian in its origin and thus expose it and render it powerless.

In the last scene of Act three, the prophet sees four chariots which were driven out upon the earth (Zech. 6:1-8). It is very much like the vision in the book of Revelation of four horsemen who ride out to bring judgment upon the earth (Rev. 6:1-8). The number four is the symbol of universality, and the four riders are sent out to bring judgment upon the whole world.

Thus the curtain rings down on the great drama of redemption. It is God's symbolic play of how to find the way back to Him—first by cleansing, then the filling of the Holy Spirit, then the putting away of lawlessness and hypocrisy, and finally the judgment of the entire earth.

Chapter 6 of Zechariah closes with a prophetic vision of the crowning of the One whose name is the Branch, and it is said of Him: "He shall grow up in his place, and he shall build the temple of the Lord. It is he who shall build the temple of the Lord, and shall bear royal honor, and shall sit and rule upon his throne" (6:12,13).

The true temple, as we have seen, is the church of the

living God, and this scene depicts the building of that great dwelling place of God by the Spirit, which Jesus, the great King-Priest, is building to the glory of His Father.

Chapter 7 marks the beginning of the last division of the book. Here God speaks in a different form, for instead of visions He addresses the prophet directly. The theme of the section is found in chapter 8, verse 3: "Thus says the Lord: I will return to Zion, and will dwell in the midst of Jerusalem, and Jerusalem shall be called the faithful city, and the mountain of the Lord of hosts, the holy mountain."

The historical setting for this message of hope and promise was an inquiry from the people as to whether they should continue celebrating the fast which had been begun in memory of the burning of Jerusalem in the fifth month of the year. God's answer was to point out that such fasts had been instituted not by divine command but solely on the initiative of the people. They were reminded that what God sought for was justice and mercy rather than the observance of self-appointed ritual. The inference was clear that had they been obedient the occasion for this fast would never have occurred. Despite the shameful record of the people's failure, God promises that when they walk in obedience and return to Him He shall turn the fasts into feasts to such a degree that all the nations around will envy the prosperity of Jerusalem and: "In those days ten men from the nations of every tongue shall take hold of the robe of a Jew, saying 'Let us go with you, for we have heard that God is with you' " (8:23).

In chapters 9-11 the prophet continues his description of the means by which God will return to His people, but this time in prophetic poetry very much in the style of Isaiah or Ezekiel. First he predicts an invasion of Israel during which Damascus, Tyre, and Sidon, and the cities of Philistia would be captured, but Jerusalem would not be attacked. This was historically fulfilled by the coming of Alexander the Great who captured Damascus and, after a siege of seven months, overthrew Tyre. He then marched against Gaza and Philistia, razing the cities to the ground; but though he passed by Jerusalem he did not attack it. Thus Zechariah's prophecy was fulfilled. In 9:9 his prophetic vision predicts the actual appearance of the divine king in Jerusalem: "Rejoice greatly, O daughter of Zion! Shout aloud, O daughter of Jerusalem! Lo, your king comes to you; triumphant and victorious is he, humble and riding on an ass, on a colt the foal of an ass." Matthew 21 records the fulfillment of this when Jesus sent His disciples to find a colt and an ass and mounted the colt to ride in triumph through the streets of Jerusalem with the people crying, "Blessed is he who comes in the name of the Lord!" Luke tells us that as He drew near Jerusalem He wept as He looked out over the impenitent city and said these remarkable words: "Would that even today you knew the things that make for peace! But now they are hid from your eyes" (Luke 19:42).

The remainder of Zechariah 9 is a prediction of victory for the sons of Judah over the sons of Greece, and many Bible scholars feel it speaks of the Maccabean uprising and victory of the Jews over Antiochus Epiphanes.

In chapter 10 the prophet looks ahead to describe the final victory of the people of God. The promise is specific: "Though I scattered them among the nations, yet in far countries they shall remember me, and with their children they shall live and return. I will bring them home from the land of Egypt, and gather them from Assyria; and I will bring them to the land of Gilead and to Lebanon, till there is no room for them" (10:9,10).

But in chapter 11 the prophet returns to a day during which a fire of judgment will devour the people and spoil the glory of the false shepherds. Many take this to be a description of the Roman conquest of Israel and the subjugation of the priesthood under Roman rule. Then the prophet is called upon to act out the role of the Good Shepherd who holds in His hands two staffs, named Grace and Union. This true Shepherd then rejects the false shepherds and is in turn rejected by the people. The staff labeled Grace is broken in half and the Shepherd is given His wages, consisting of 30 shekels of silver which are cast into the treasury (in Hebrew it is the word *potter*). This is a remarkable foreview of the betrayal by Judas for 30 shekels of silver, which were ultimately paid to the potter for the field in which the body of Judas was buried.

After this the prophet, still enacting the role of the Good Shepherd, broke the second staff labeled Union and thus symbolized the breakup of the nation and its ultimate dispersion among the nations of the world.

The prophet is then told to play the role of a false shepherd, for Jehovah says: "For lo, I am raising up in the land a shepherd who does not care for the perishing, or seek the wandering, or heal the maimed, or nourish the sound, but devours the flesh of the fat ones, tearing off even their hoofs" (11:16). Very likely Jesus had this passage in mind when He said to the blinded Pharisees of His day: "I have come in my Father's name, and you do not receive me; if another comes in his own name, him you will receive" (John 5:43).

This false shepherd is the one whom the apostle Paul calls the man of sin who shall be received as the Messiah but turns out to be the anti-Messiah, the one we know as the antichrist (see 2 Thess. 2:1-4). It is remarkable that today, when many are falling into the error of anti-Christian cults, they do so because they have first rejected an opportunity to hear the truth. The result is they are allowed to believe a lie, just as Paul warns will be the case in the last days.

Zechariah 12-14 constitute the last vision of the prophet and his final description of how God finds a way to return to His people. It opens with these words: "Lo, I am about to make Jerusalem a cup of reeling to all the peoples round about; it will be against Judah also in the siege against Jerusalem. On that day I will make Jerusalem a heavy stone for all the peoples; all who lift it shall grievously hurt themselves. And all the nations of the earth will come together against it" (12:2,3). According to this word the darkest days for Jerusalem lie yet ahead. It shall become a burden to all nations, a grievous stone of stumbling. Against it the peoples of the nations shall be gathered together, for Zechariah informs us that God will not allow Himself to be ignored, but the ultimate breakthrough will come by the actions of divine grace.

"And I will pour out on the house of David and the inhabitants of Jerusalem a spirit of compassion and supplication, so that, when they look on him whom they have pierced, they shall mourn for him, as one mourns for an only child, and weep bitterly over him, as one weeps over a first-born" (12:10).

After the mourning comes the cleansing of the people and the setting aside of the idols of the land. Then prophecy will be brought to an end, for there shall be no need for further prediction. The time has come when all that the prophets have uttered shall be fulfilled.

In chapter 14 the prophet returns again to the vision of the destruction of Jerusalem, and describes how the nations surround it and the city is taken and plundered, and at that time he declares: "Then the Lord will go forth and fight against those nations as when he fights on a day of battle. On that day his feet shall stand on the Mount of Olives which lies before Jerusalem on the east; and the Mount of Olives shall be split in two from east to west by a very wide valley; so that one half of the Mount shall withdraw northward, and the other half southward. And the valley of my mountains shall be stopped up, for the valley of the mountains shall touch the side of it; and you shall flee as you fled from the earthquake in the days of Uzziah king of Judah. Then the Lord your God will come, and all the holy ones with him" (14:3-5).

Geologists have long known that a great earth fault runs through the Mount of Olives. There is certainly coming a day when the mountain shall be split in half and the armies of the nations that assault it shall flee in terror.

The prophetic vision goes on to say: "On that day living waters shall flow out from Jerusalem, half of them to the eastern sea and half of them to the western sea; it shall continue in summer as in winter. And the Lord will become king over all the earth; on that day the Lord will be one and his name one" (14:8,9).

This accords with the description of Ezekiel and Joel and depicts the glory of the earth in the days when God shall reign, through His Son, as King over all the earth. The book then closes with these beautiful words: "And on that day there shall be inscribed on the bells of the horses, 'Holy to the Lord.' And the pots in the house of the Lord shall be as the bowls before the altar; and every pot in Jerusalem and Judah shall be sacred to the Lord of hosts, so that all who sacrifice may come and take of them and boil the flesh of the sacrifice in them. And there shall no longer be a trader in the house of the Lord of hosts on that day" (14:20,21).

Every commonplace thing is yet to be made holy unto the Lord. Have you realized that that is what God is promising you? Every moment of your life, every commonplace thing, shall be touched with the glory of His presence when He is in the center of your life. Someday it will be visibly true on earth, but it can be spiritually true of those who open their hearts and enthrone the King of Glory as Lord in their lives right now!

MALACHI

This last book of the Old Testament is separated in time from the first book of the New Testament by a period of more than 400 years. After the ministry of Malachi the heavens fell silent, and no prophet came to Israel and no further Scriptures were written. History, of course, was still going on, and remarkable things were taking place in Israel among the Jews. New institutions were being formed that appear in the opening of the New Testament, but none of this is recorded in sacred history.

As we have already seen, the Jews did not return from Babyylon in one great happy throng. There was a drawn out, straggling return, consisting of several groups. The first one, led by Zerubbabel, was in 535 B.C. After building their own homes they began to lay the foundations of the Temple, but when this work slowed to a halt it was Haggai's ministry 15 years later that stirred them up to carry on the work.

The Temple was completed during the ministry of Zechariah, and during this time Ezra the priest led another group back from Babylon. Finally the last return was accomplished under Nehemiah, who in 445 B.C. began to lay the walls of the city of Jerusalem.

It was shortly after Nehemiah finished his task that the prophet Malachi appeared on the scene. If the prophecy of Malachi is read in connection with the historical events of Nehemiah, it is clearly evident that they were contemporary.

The name *Malachi* means "my messenger." The prophecy opens with a tender and sensitive word from the Lord to the people: " 'I have loved you,' says the Lord" (1:2). This is the underlying theme of Malachi's prophecy, and forms the bright background against which is seen, in stark contrast, the darkened hearts and blinded minds of the people.

Though the Temple was now completed and the walls of Jerusalem were rebuilt, still the people were not enjoying the promised period of blessing and prosperity which Haggai and Zechariah had predicted. As a consequence, their reply to the Lord's vow of love was: "How have you loved us?" The structure of the book of Malachi is here revealed, for again and again God declares His expectation of love from them in return for His love of them, and seven times the people reply, in effect: "How have we fallen short? We do not see any failure on our part." Here is a callous people who have become so indifferent and unresponsive to God that, in perfect sincerity, they can reply, "What do you mean—why do you say such things to us? We do not see any evidence of love on your part."

God's answer to their question, How have you loved us? is to remind them that His love dated from the very beginning of the race, as evidenced in the patriarchs, Jacob and Esau: " 'Is not Esau Jacob's brother?' says the Lord. 'Yet I have loved Jacob but I have hated Esau' " (1:2). He goes on to point out that the history of Edom, the nation descended from Esau, is quite different from the story of Jacob and Israel.

If we had known these two men we probably would have loved Esau and hated Jacob, for Jacob was the schemer, the operator, the untrustworthy rascal. Esau was the outdoor man, hearty, open, frank and strong. Of the two he appears naturally to be much the better man; but in effect God says, "I love Jacob, because in his heart is a hunger for deeper things than life affords." Jacob wants something more than what is on the surface. That always draws out the heart of God. Esau was a despiser of his birthright and cared nothing for spiritual matters.

God's love for Israel should have drawn from them a response of love in return, but through Malachi God charges the people with their failure to return His love: "A son honors his father, and a servant his master. If then I am a father, where is my honor? And if I am a master, where is my fear? says the Lord of hosts to you, O priests, who despise my name" (1:6). These charges against the priests, which run on through chapter 2, verse 9, reveal in detail how the priests committed sacrilege in offering polluted food on the altar of Jehovah, and manifested greed and covetousness in that none was found willing to open the doors of the Temple without pay; and finally displayed contempt for the whole sacrificial system which manifested itself in sniffing at it as a great weariness of the flesh.

To these accusations the priests respond with great resentment, asking again and again, "How have we?" The punishment of the priests was that they would be made despised and abased before all the people. This is always the reaction of people to hypocrisy in the ministry. There is nothing but contempt for those who claim to be the special ministers of the Lord but whose lives deny God's ways.

In the latter part of chapter 2 the prophet details the sins of the people. The first specific sin was the mixed marriages of the people with the pagan nations around them. Throughout the history of Israel this had always led to the introduction of idolatry and ultimate depravity. These people seemed to have learned nothing from the years of captivity in Babylon, and were again beginning the same practices which had destroyed them as a nation years before.

The second sin was the prevalence of divorce. When the people asked why God did not receive their offerings any longer, the prophet replies: "And this again you do. You cover the Lord's altar with tears, with weeping and groaning because he no longer regards the offering or accepts it with favor at your hand. You ask, 'Why does he not?' Because the Lord was witness to the covenant between you and the wife of your youth, to whom you have been faithless, though she is your companion and your wife by covenant. Has not the one God made and sustained for us the spirit of life? And what does he desire? Godly offspring. So take heed to yourselves, and let none be faithless to the wife of his youth. For I hate divorce, says the Lord the God of Israel" (2:13-16).

This sounds very contemporary, does it not? Malachi had to minister to a nation in which divorce was widespread and, more than that, to a society in which moral confusion and cynicism was rampant. While indulging in easy divorce and mixed marriages, the people were, nevertheless, saying: "Every one who does evil is good in the sight of the Lord, and he delights in them." This is equivalent to what we often hear today, "God is so loving and merciful that He will not punish sin, but only bless the sinner." Even more up-to-date, some of the people of Malachi's time were asking, "Where is the God of justice?" which is to say, "God does nothing; why should we care?"

But chapter 3 contains the remarkable prediction of the coming Messiah. It begins with the words: "Behold, I send my messenger [in Hebrew that would be, "Behold, I send Malachi"] to prepare the way before me." As we discover in the book of Matthew, that "messenger" was John the Baptist. He came to prepare the way of the Lord, to announce the coming of a second Messenger from God. That second Messenger is now brought before us in Malachi's prediction: "And the Lord whom you seek will suddenly come to his temple; the messenger of the covenant in whom you delight, behold, he is coming says the Lord of hosts" (3:1). This clearly foresees the night when the Lord Jesus took wine and bread with His disciples, and holding the cup said, "This is my blood of the covenant, which is poured out for many for the forgiveness of sins" (Matt 26:28). He is clearly, then, Malachi's "messenger of the covenant."

But Malachi sees further and asks: "But who can endure the day of his coming, and who can stand when he appears? For he is like a refiner's fire and like fullers' soap; he will sit as a refiner and purifier of silver, and he will purify the sons of Levi and refine them like gold and silver, till they present right offerings to the Lord" (3:2,3).

Seeing through the centuries, the prophet describes One who will burn through the hypocrisy of the people and the outward perfunctoriness of their religion and cut through to the very heart. He will be like fullers' soap to those who are willing, cleansing them and setting all things right; and they will recognize Him because a messenger will go before Him to prepare the way. There is no mistaking the fulfillment of this in the ministry of Jesus of Nazareth.

After the great vision of the coming of Messiah, Malachi returns to the charges against the nation and calls the people to return to God that He might return to them. Again his charge is two-fold, accusing them of robbery and of blasphemy. When they respond with the inquiry: "How are we?" he shows them that they were cheating God in withholding the tithe which the law required, and were blaspheming Him by saying, in effect, "What is the use of serving God? He does not do anything for us. We do not get anything out of this, so what is the use of trying to be godly?"

But in verse 16 the spotlight is turned upon a small remnant of the people who were pleasing God. These are described thus: "Then those who feared the Lord spoke with one another; the Lord heeded and heard them, and a book of remembrance was written before him of those who feared the Lord and thought on his name" (3:16).

Notice the two things that mark their faithfulness.

First, they "spoke with one another." This does not mean that they conversed, but that they opened up with each other. They shared with one another. They encouraged each other. They confessed their weakness and prayed with one another.

All that was on the horizontal level. But there was also the vertical: They "thought on his name." That is forever the great resource of the people of God. The name of God stands for all that He is, as when we sign a check we lay on the line all that we are to the amount of the check. These believers in Malachi's day thought on the name of God. They did not reckon on visible resources, or count on special gimmicks or gadgets to make their work acceptable in God's sight, but they counted on God Himself. Therefore the promise of Jehovah is: "They shall be mine, says the Lord of hosts, my special possession on the day when I act, and I will spare them as a man spares his son who serves him. Then once more you shall distinguish between the righteous and the wicked, between one who serves God and one who does not serve him" (3:17,18).

The final vision of the prophet is of the coming of "the great and terrible day of the Lord." It shall be when "the sun of righteousness shall rise, with healing in its wings" (4:2). For those who have refused Him there is a terrible burning, but for those who receive Him there is healing. "You shall go forth leaping like calves from the stall. And you shall tread down the wicked, for they will be ashes under the soles of your feet, on the day when I act, says the Lord of hosts" (4:2,3).

The final prediction is of the coming of Elijah: "Behold, I will send you Elijah the prophet before the great and terrible day of the Lord comes. And he will turn the hearts of fathers to their children and the hearts of children to their fathers, lest I come and smite the land with a curse" (4:5,6).

Matthew records how this last verse was a source of

trouble to the disciples of Jesus, for they said to Him:
"Then why do the scribes say that first Elijah must come?"
The Lord's answer was, "Elijah has already come, and
they did not know him" (17:10,12). He saw the look of
astonishment on their faces and made it clear that it was
John the Baptist who came "in the spirit and power of
Elijah" (Luke 1:17) and fulfilled his ministry in that initial
coming. Yet Jesus stated this in such a way as to leave the
clear inference that Elijah the prophet would actually
come before the glorious appearing. Many identify the
two witnesses of Revelation 11 as Elijah and Moses,
though it is difficult to be dogmatic about that point.

But it is not without significance that at the end of all
the literature of the Old Testament the last word is:
"curse." The prophecy of Malachi begins: "I have loved
you, says the Lord." But it ends with the warning that if
the message of love is not received the only alternative is a
curse.

Compare that with the last word of the New Testament. Leaving out the final benediction, the last word is
the name above all names: "Come, Lord Jesus!" That is
God's answer to the curse. Jesus has redeemed us from
the curse of the law, being made a curse for us! Thus the
full answer of God is grace and love which pours out even
more blessing, despite man's sin, that we might be
brought at last into the light and knowledge of Christ.
Thus the supreme task of the Christian is to learn to think
upon His name and enjoy the "unsearchable riches of
Christ" (Eph. 3:8).

So the great message of the prophets draws to a close.
These sturdy men of God, coming from all walks of life,
have been called into activity to reveal the character of
God's heart. Through all their severe words and forceful
utterances, there runs the revelation that God does not
delight in judgment but uses it only that He might waken
His people to the reality of where they really are before

Him. But the final word is never one of law but of grace.

Finally, across the corridors of the centuries, there is always the final scene of glory, where the Son of Righteousness rises with healing in His wings. Thus when Malachi lays down his pen, the next word to be heard from the divine lips is this: "The book of the genealogy of Jesus Christ, the son of David, the son of Abraham" (Matt. 1:1).